ABOUT THE AUTHOR

Sarah 'Sassy' Smith is a trainer, coach, speaker, and educator known for her work raising awareness of invisible cognitive differences like multisensory aphantasia. She is the founder of Aphantasia Academy and creator of the Unseen Minds Practitioner® training, the first CPD-certified course in the UK designed specifically for practitioners working with clients who experience multisensory aphantasia, SDAM, anauralia, anendophasia, and alexithymia. She combines academic rigour and lived experience with a deep commitment to real-world impact.

What sets Sassy's work apart is her dual lens. She not only teaches about these differences, but she also lives with them. Her own experience of going through therapy without mental imagery, internal dialogue or emotionally rich memory gives her a uniquely compassionate perspective on what many clients are quietly struggling with behind the scenes. Her mission is to help therapists recognise when the models they rely on might be misaligned with how a client's mind actually works, and to offer practical, respectful ways to adapt.

Unseen Minds

A therapist's guide to multisensory aphantasia and invisible cognitive differences

Sassy Smith

Second edition July 2026
1
First published February 2026 by Aphantasia Academy Ltd

A catalogue edition of this book is available at the British Library

This book contains advice and information relating to mental health care. It should not be used to replace the advice of a qualified doctor or other trained health professional. All efforts have been made to assure the accuracy of the information contained in this book as of the day of publication. The publisher and author disclaim liability for any medical outcomes that may occur as a result of applying the methods suggested in this book and any actions are taken entirely at the reader's own risk.

For more information visit: aphantasiaacademy.com

the aphantasia academy
education & training for professionals

Contents

Contents

Introduction

Unseen Minds is a book I never planned to write and yet, in many ways, I was always going to.

This book was born out of personal frustration, confusion, and the deeply disorienting experience of not being understood in therapy. Not because I wasn't willing, but because my mind simply didn't work in the way therapy expected it to.

I came into therapy already knowing that I had aphantasia, SDAM (severely deficient autobiographical memory), anauralia, anendophasia, and alexithymia. I wasn't confused about how my mind worked, as I had spent years understanding it, living with it, and learning how it shaped my experience of the world.

What I hadn't expected was that the therapists I turned to for support had either no or very limited understanding of these cognitive differences.

That's when I realised that the problem wasn't with me, it was with the training, with the assumptions around how our inner worlds work, and with the lack of knowledge and understanding. It was with therapeutic models that simply haven't caught up with the full diversity of human minds.

This experience took me from being a coach and practitioner to a woman determined to make sure no one had to sit through therapy thinking they were broken or not believed, when, in fact, they were simply misunderstood.

This book is my invitation to you to see what's been hidden, to recognise what's been missing, and to gently explore how you might work more effectively with clients whose minds don't fit the mold that therapy was built around.

This isn't a textbook or a manual. Instead, it's a conversation, a starting point and a guide to what could be.

Who this book is for

This book is primarily written for counsellors, psychotherapists, and other mental health professionals who want to expand their practice to include neurodivergent clients, especially those with cognitive profiles that are often invisible and deeply misunderstood.

If you've ever sat with a client who didn't respond to visualisation, struggled with memory-based work, or seemed emotionally flat despite your best efforts, this book is for you.

If you've ever wondered why some clients just don't "get" inner child work, can't connect with parts, or fail to respond to imagery or future pacing techniques, this book is for you.

If you're committed to inclusivity, accessibility, and client-centred practice, and you want to grow your understanding of how different minds experience therapy, this book is for you.

Nor is it only for therapists.

This book is also for coaches, educators, wellbeing practitioners, and even those who are just beginning to suspect they might have one or more of the cognitive differences described here. If you've recently discovered the term *aphantasia* or stumbled across *SDAM*, this book will help you understand what it all means, especially in the context of personal growth and mental health.

It isn't designed to replace clinical training, but to spark awareness. It will not give you all the tools, but it will show you why you need them.

Most importantly, it will point you to the path forward, towards the specialised training that can transform your work and the lives of the clients you serve.

How to use this book

This is an interactive book, and it's been written with real-world application in mind.

Each chapter introduces a key concept that makes up the cluster of multisensory and cognitive processing differences: aphantasia, SDAM (Severely Deficient Autobiographical Memory), anauralia, anendophasia, and alexithymia.

You'll find short reflective exercises and practice-based prompts throughout. These are invitations to pause, reflect, and reconsider, not academic tasks. To look again at how you work, and who you might be missing.

Some chapters include brief case examples, drawn from either my own lived experience or composite client stories. These are designed to help you "feel into" what therapy might look like from the client's point of view.

I encourage you to:

- Keep a journal or notepad to write down your reflections.
- Pause at the end of each chapter to consider what has shifted in your understanding.

- Resist the urge to diagnose, this book isn't about pathologising but about understanding.

If, by the final chapter, you've found yourself rethinking just one part of your practice, then this book has done its job.

If you're ready to go deeper, the final chapter will show you how.

Chapter 1

Where it all began

For months, I'd known something wasn't quite right. I couldn't name it, but I could feel it. There was a tightness in my chest, a churning in my stomach, and a fog that sat like a veil across my thoughts. Nights became restless and I would lie in bed for hours, eyes wide open in the darkness, staring at nothing. In the morning, as I woke from what little sleep I'd had, I could feel a strange energy in my mind, as though thoughts were spinning, and spiralling, but there was just silence. No racing thoughts to tell me what was worrying me. No stream of consciousness. Just a tense, humming stillness, like something was trying to form just out of reach.

Knowing something was wrong, I did what I'd always done, I tried to understand it. Every morning, I sat down with my journal and attempted to write my way to clarity. My logical mind worked overtime, dissecting every element of my situation. I knew what the problem was on paper, yet nothing about the emotional intensity made sense. Why this situation? Why now? Why was I spiralling when, on the surface, everything looked so normal? It just made no sense and the harder I dug to try to get to the root of the problem, the deeper I fell into the blackest of holes.

When journaling didn't help, I turned to my usual coping tools. I meditated, I practised mindfulness, I tried grounding exercises, and breathwork. Yet these tools that had previously been helpful to me just weren't working. Still, I hoped something would shift.

Then, one day, I just broke. I couldn't get out of bed and the spiralling I'd felt for weeks turned to the heaviest weight. Tears came in waves I couldn't explain. Panic attacks started without warning, and I was clearly no longer managing. I couldn't work and I could barely function. I was broken and I didn't know how to put myself back together again.

I knew I needed help and not in a vague, future-oriented way, but right now, urgently. I needed someone who could help me make sense of the overwhelm, the burnout, the strange disconnect between knowing what was happening and not being able to feel my way through it. I needed someone who could help me to dig deep enough to identify and understand the silent spiralling thoughts. Someone who could get me past my logical knowledge of the situation and closer to understanding what I was feeling and unable to name. Someone who could help me out of a depression I'd never experienced before.

I met with a therapist whose background and profile gave me confidence that I was going to get the help I needed. During our initial call, I explained that I live with multisensory aphantasia, severely deficient autobiographical memory (SDAM), alexithymia and anendophasia.

If you've never heard of those terms, you're not alone, most people haven't, but I had learned enough by this point to explain them clearly.

I said that I couldn't visualise, that I had no mental pictures, and no internal senses. That my childhood memories were inaccessible to me, just facts or the stories that others told about my life. I said that I don't have an inner monologue and experience thoughts wordlessly, without hearing them in my mind.

I explained that, logically, I was very aware of the cause and the events that had led to me feeling this way, but that I didn't understand why I wasn't coping with that situation. That living with these cognitive differences was making it difficult to understand what I was thinking and why it was hitting me so hard.

I was seeking support to understand why I was so emotionally overwhelmed by a present-day situation that wouldn't normally have affected me. What I really needed was someone who could help me find the thoughts that I couldn't hear, so I could address them and move on.

Someone who could help me uncover what was triggering this reaction and how I could process and heal from that.

My therapist hadn't heard of any of these terms before, but was warm, curious, and professional. I felt hopeful that, even without prior knowledge, we could find a way to work together.

Sadly, that isn't what happened.

In our very first session, I was invited to talk about my childhood. "I can't access those memories," I said gently. They nodded and asked, "Can you see yourself as a child and imagine yourself in your bedroom?" I sighed. "That's not something I can do" I said.

They nodded again and said that we would try something else. "Thinking about the moments when you feel yourself spiralling, what are you thinking? What is your inner Sassy saying to you? "I don't know, I can't 'hear' those thoughts," I reminded them. "My thoughts don't come through as speech."

I would explain, repeatedly, that I couldn't do what they were asking. That I had no inner child to visualise, no inner voice to interrogate and no inner world to explore in the way they meant. Each time, they'd rephrase the same questions and offer the same techniques, as if repetition might loosen something.

It didn't, and that pattern continued for all our sessions.

We would talk about how planning for what I could do to get me out of the situation would help me to move forward, but I had already done that. I'd already decided on the course of action I needed to take to remove myself from the situation. I had a plan and was ready to start putting it into practice but first I needed to overcome the crushing depression, overwhelming anxiety, and all too frequent panic attacks so I was well enough to put that plan into action.

I needed to find a way to uncover my thoughts, deal with them and move on.

They were trying their best. I honestly believe that. They were kind, well-intentioned, and clearly cared about helping me, but the tools they relied on were incompatible with my mind. Since they didn't understand my internal experience, or perhaps didn't fully believe it, our sessions became a painful, frustrating mismatch.

By the fourth session, I had checked out. I was no longer engaging and, if I'm honest, I was just there because I had six sessions and felt obligated to turn up. I've often wondered if they had also checked out by then too.

I left that therapeutic relationship feeling more broken than when I entered it. Now I wasn't just struggling, I was starting to believe I was unfixable and that I'd never be well again.

Looking back, I see it clearly now. It wasn't their fault; they always demonstrated a willingness to want to help me, but they just didn't know how to.

Like most therapists, they had never been trained to recognise or adapt for minds that don't operate in imagery, memory, or inner dialogue. They had never been taught that some clients can't feel or step into memories, can't *see* safe places, and don't have an internal voice to talk to. That for some of us, uncovering our thoughts can be difficult, and without that knowledge, they couldn't adapt. They were working with only the tools they had, and those tools just didn't work for me.

It wasn't until later when I began speaking with others like me that I realised how common this experience was.

At first, I thought my experience was an unfortunate one-off, that I'd simply found myself matched with a therapist who wasn't the right fit. So, I went looking for stories like mine, hoping to find someone who could say, "Yes, I've been there, and here's what helped."

I searched forums, support groups, and professional directories. I read every post I could find that mentioned aphantasia, SDAM, no inner monologue, or alexithymia. I looked for recommendations, and I typed keywords into therapist and counsellor registers.

Every time, though, my searches proved fruitless. It didn't matter which directory I tried, there just wasn't anyone who said that they understood these cognitive differences.

What I found instead were stories just like mine. Stories from people who sat in rooms trying to comply, trying to explain, and slowly giving up. Clients who left therapy not only feeling unsupported, but also deeply ashamed. Some were told they were dissociating, others were accused of resisting, a few were labelled as emotionally avoidant.

Like me, most said that they just checked out, and they gave up. Others who quietly left, ghosting their therapists when reminded that they were due to book further sessions.

Time and again I read comments from people saying that they left feeling even more broken. This was especially true for those who, at the time, had no idea that they even had a different way of thinking and experiencing the world.

Scattered amongst the 'horror' stories, I found glimmers of hope. Therapists who hadn't heard of aphantasia but had listened. Professionals who, even without training, had adjusted their language and approach to meet their clients where they were. There weren't many, but they existed, and they were making a difference.

Those early threads of possibility gave me something I hadn't felt in a long time: purpose. I remember thinking that I was going to have to fix myself, and once I'd done that, I was going to 'fix' therapy for people like me.

I threw myself into learning. I revisited everything I thought I knew about therapy, first from a client perspective, and then from a practitioner. I undertook counselling training, not because I planned to become a therapist in the traditional sense, but because I wanted to understand the frameworks, models, and assumptions from the inside.

What I found confirmed what I had already sensed. Most therapeutic techniques are designed around minds that are visual, emotionally expressive, and rich in inner narrative. Those models depend on memory, imagery, sensory processing, and verbal emotional awareness.

They are not built for people like me...but they *could* be if therapists knew, if therapists understood and if therapists were trained to adapt.

I set about developing the training that would help therapists to know, to understand and how to adapt. It became my mission and hours of research and practical application led to the launch of the specialist training that is now the Unseen Minds Practitioner® programme, the UK's first training programme designed specifically for therapists.

Therapists who've completed this have come away with a whole new level of understanding to help them to connect with people like me. To support us to feel seen, understood and heard. Some have said that it's the most valuable training they've taken, since qualifying, and that they wish they'd discovered it sooner.

Many have said that they wished they had been more aware of these cognitive differences and that was one of the main drivers for me writing this book.

This isn't a full methodology, nor a substitute for training, and it's certainly not an accusation. It's a guide, and insight into what so many clients have struggled to express.

It's a way of showing therapists what might be happening beneath the surface of confusion, resistance, or shutdown. Most importantly, it's a way of opening the door to therapeutic practice that is more inclusive, more flexible, and more aware.

People like me are already in your rooms and we've always been there. We're thoughtful, sensitive, analytical, and emotionally present but cognitively different.

You don't need to change everything, but you do need to see us and that's what this book is for.

Now that you understand my journey, let's explore how these assumptions about our inner worlds shape therapy itself.

Reflective practice

Before you turn the page, I invite you to pause with the following:

1. *Have you ever had a client who didn't respond to visualisation, memory recall, or parts work in the way you expected? What interpretation did you make at the time?*
2. *Have you ever gently insisted that a client "just try" to picture something, even after they said they couldn't?*
3. *Have you considered that difference, not resistance, might be behind certain moments of therapeutic mismatch?*
4. *How does my story sit with you? What thoughts or feelings does it bring up?*
5. *What would it mean for your practice if some of your clients can't visualise, recall their childhood, or access an inner voice and they started to 'check out' in your sessions?*

You don't need to have all the answers now, but if these questions stir something in you, a sense of curiosity, reflection, even discomfort, then you are exactly the person this book was written for.

Chapter 2

When therapy assumes a rich inner world

We grow up with messages everywhere that our minds should be full of pictures, voices, and richly detailed memories. Children's books ask us to imagine dragons, fairies, and magical kingdoms. School exercises prompt us to "picture your perfect day" or "use the blackboard in your mind." to solve complex maths equations. Films portray memory as vivid flashbacks, often layered with narrative voiceover, the inner monologue made audible. Self-help literature tells us to "visualise your goals," while meditation apps begin with, "Close your eyes and imagine yourself..."

Visualisation and inner speech are so normalised that we rarely question them. In fact, they're not just seen as normal, they're considered essential tools for personal development. Research into sports and performance psychology frequently highlights the benefits of mental rehearsal. Studies show that athletes who visualise their routine often perform better. Motivational speakers and business coaches encourage clients to create vision boards, mentally rehearse success, and engage their senses to manifest their desired future.

There is robust evidence for these practices. Imagery-based mental training can enhance motor learning, increase confidence, and strengthen emotional resilience. What happens, though, when a person can't picture a scene, imagine a movement, or hear their own internal voice narrating a task?

Where does that leave people who simply don't have access to that kind of inner world?

The answer, sadly, is often exclusion, not by design or intention but by assumption.

This cultural backdrop creates a foundation that quietly infiltrates therapeutic practice. It's never said outright, but it's always there, this quiet assumption that everyone has access to an inner world of pictures, inner voices, rich emotional recall, and sensory experience.

It's not unique to one modality or method, it shows up everywhere; in scripts, in training manuals, in CPD workshops, in the phrases we repeat to our clients and ourselves.

"Talk to the part of you that's afraid." "Go back to the moment that memory was formed." "What were you thinking at that moment?"

Far from careless, these instructions are thoughtful, therapeutic, and often transformative. They are shaped, though, by a particular world view, one that assumes everyone *can* imagine, recall, visualise, and connect in the same way.

That becomes a problem when the client in front of you simply can't do the things you are asking of them. It also becomes a problem when it assumes that the absence of this inner world means that something is wrong.

When a client struggles to visualise their childhood home or talk to their inner child, we often interpret this as resistance, avoidance, trauma, or a relational block. When a client can't recall the emotional tone of a significant life event, we may conclude that they're not accessing the work deeply enough, or that dissociation is at play.

Sometimes those assumptions are accurate. Sometimes, though, those responses stem from cognitive differences that may have been there since birth, with nothing psychological about them at all. Differences that your client might not even be aware of.

When therapy has been shaped by a single dominant model of the inner world, these differences become invisible, unseen, leading to a mismatch and the potential for a breakdown in the therapeutic relationship.

My experience of this isn't unique, with many people like me saying that therapy left them feeling "like a failure", "broken" or that it could never work for them.

If your client can't do what you're asking them, maybe they aren't shutting you out, or being resistant, maybe they're giving you the most honest version of their internal experience but therapy, as it's commonly practised, doesn't always know how to receive that.

Claire's story

Claire is a project manager for a large banking firm. Throughout her career she prided herself on her ability to handle workplace feedback, and other people's personalities with ease. She was known for being calm, reasonable, and professional, able to take constructive criticism in her stride and resolve conflict with clarity. That changed when a new colleague joined one of her project teams, and with them came a wave of unexpected reactions. In meetings, when this person spoke sharply or offered critique, Claire would feel flooded with emotions. Her chest would tighten, her stomach would churn, and she would find herself rattled for hours afterwards. She didn't understand why because nothing overt had happened and the things he was saying weren't anything she hadn't dealt with before. There was no confrontation, no aggression, no inappropriate comment but she still felt a consistent, visceral reaction that didn't match the surface of the interaction.

Claire was asked who the colleague reminded her of, she couldn't answer. Not because she didn't want to, but because there was simply nothing there. No memory, no image, no story, just the same blank fog she always felt when trying to recall the past.

When her therapist asked her to describe what she was thinking in those moments, she struggled again. She knew there was something that she was reacting to, but she just couldn't access the thoughts behind the feelings.

Claire didn't know that cognitive differences like SDAM, aphantasia, or anendophasia existed. All she knew was that therapy had become a space where she couldn't explain herself and that it was unlikely to ever be effective for her.

Claire's story isn't unique. Here's how it often begins: You've been working with a client for a few sessions. You feel there's a good alliance, great rapport and they're engaged, present, and reflective. Then you introduce something that relies on internal imagery or sensory recall, perhaps a visualisation or a memory-based intervention.

You say, “Let’s go back to that moment. What do you see?”

They hesitate, or they say, “When you say ‘see’ what do you mean?” Or maybe they start to talk about what they ‘see’ in a way that sounds like they are reading from a shopping list. Factual things lacking in rich detail or emotion. Or maybe they just say, “I don’t know”, look confused by your question and talk about having “a dreadful memory”.

So, you rephrase or encourage. You offer some structure. “Imagine you’re stepping into that moment, just observing it from the outside. Like you’re watching it happen. What images, or sensations are present?”

Still nothing.

At this point you make a mental note that they seem uncomfortable with the exercise, possibly resistant or even a trauma-related blockage. You file it under ‘needs more time’ and move on. Or you try to find other ways to help them to uncover and understand the ‘blockage’ that seems to make them even more confused.

What might your client be experiencing, though? They may be thinking:

- “Is this how therapy is supposed to work? Am I doing it wrong?”
- “If I don’t feel anything, does that mean I’m numb?”
- “Should I just say something to move it along? I could just make something up”
- “Maybe I’m broken.”

Right there, without rupture, without raised voices, something vital is lost: the sense that the therapist sees the client clearly.

Clients with multisensory aphantasia, anauralia, anendophasia, or SDAM often sit in therapy rooms silently questioning themselves. They've followed the instructions, and they've tried the exercises, but when nothing shows up, they're left with a difficult internal narrative.

They may conclude they are doing therapy badly because they are failing at introspection. They may feel that they are too "in their head," emotionally blocked, or irreparably broken.

What they don't realise, and what therapists often haven't been taught to consider, is that the barrier lies in the wiring, not the will.

In supervision, we're often taught to look for what lies beneath. When a client doesn't engage with an intervention, we ask, "What's being avoided?" We look for what the behaviour is protecting. We wonder what attachment dynamic is being replayed. Rarely do we ask, "What if this simply isn't how their mind works?"

Therapists are trained to map emotional responses onto a landscape of trauma, attachment, and defence. We're less often encouraged to look at *cognitive processing styles* as a foundational element of how a client engages, or doesn't, with therapeutic methods. The result is that genuine difference is often read as dysfunction. It is labelled, interpreted, or explained away using familiar frames. We don't question the tool, we question the client's readiness, openness, or depth of work. What if it's the tool that's the mismatch? What if your client doesn't need to be "encouraged" to connect with their younger self, but needs you to find a way of working that doesn't rely on internal imagery or their inner world at all?

Most therapists begin their professional journey with a deep commitment to helping others. They study diligently, reflect honestly, and build therapeutic relationships with care. Training equips them with a broad range of theories and techniques from psychodynamic thinking to person-centred principles, trauma frameworks to CBT protocols.

There is guidance on working with dissociation, neurodevelopmental differences, and relational dynamics, but there's a notable gap in the curriculum.

Very few training programmes teach therapists how to work with clients whose inner worlds are simply built differently. You might be taught to explore memory, but not what to do when a client can't access autobiographical memory at all. You may learn to work with parts, but not what it means when a client doesn't hear an inner voice. You're guided to use imagery, metaphor, and emotional recall but rarely shown how to support clients who can't visualise, can't name what they feel, or don't "re-live" the past in sensory ways.

These experiences are far from fringe. They simply go unnamed in most training, and when something isn't named, it becomes invisible to the client and to the therapist alike.

At this stage it's important to understand that this isn't a failing on your part. It's simply a gap in the system. A gap that doesn't recognise, or support you for:

- People who don't visualise
- People who don't hear an internal monologue
- People who don't emotionally "re-live" memories
- People who can't access their life memories.

- People who can't name or feel their emotions in a typical way

You've been trying to support clients with the best tools and knowledge available to you. It's even possible that you've been intuitively trying to adapt, even without knowing what you were adapting for. Maybe you've even sensed when something didn't quite fit, but you didn't have the words to explain why that might be.

As I've said before, this book is here to fill in those gaps, never to shame your practice, and to give you language, insight, and starting points that enhance what you already do well.

Once you see these invisible differences, you can't unsee them, and once you start adapting intentionally, clients who previously checked out or quietly disappeared may finally find a way to stay.

Reflective practice

Noticing Your Own Framework

Set aside ten to fifteen minutes to sit with the following questions. You may wish to journal your responses, discuss them in supervision, or use them as prompts for your own professional development planning.

1. *Which therapeutic tools or techniques do I use that rely on the client having internal imagery, emotional memory, or inner speech? Think beyond formal interventions and consider the language and metaphors you use.*
2. *When a client says, "I don't see anything," or "I'm not sure how I feel," how do I usually respond? Do I assume resistance? Do I reframe? Do I pause and explore further?*
3. *Have I ever interpreted a client's cognitive difference as emotional flatness or disconnection? What might I have missed?*
4. *How comfortable am I sitting with not knowing, especially when a tool I usually trust doesn't work? What do I reach for in those moments?*
5. *What would it mean to practise therapy that centres the client's way of experiencing the world, even if it looks nothing like my own? How might that change my sense of confidence, flexibility, or creativity as a practitioner?*

The work of becoming a more inclusive therapist is never about perfection, it's about attention. The more willing you are to question your tools, the more space you make for the client who has never quite fit into them.

Chapter 3

Aphantasia: a mind without pictures

Most people, when asked to imagine a beach, can conjure images, ranging from black and white, photo realistic or even intensely vivid images across all senses. For some imagining a beach includes a sense of golden sand beneath their feet, the rhythmic sound of waves, the warmth of the sun on their skin. For those with aphantasia, being asked to visualise is impossible, not merely difficult. When they close their eyes, there are no images. Their mind's eye is absent rather than dim.

The term *aphantasia* was first coined by Professor Adam Zeman in 2015 following a study at the University of Exeter. The name comes from the Greek "a" (without) and "phantasia" (imagination or appearance). While the phenomenon was first described more than a century ago, it is only recently that it has gained serious scientific attention. Aphantasia refers specifically to the inability to voluntarily create mental imagery, especially visual imagery. People with this difference can't 'see' a beach, a face, or a sunset in their mind, no matter how hard they try.

The implications of this go far beyond visual imagination, especially in therapy.

Multisensory aphantasia and cognitive modalities affected

Although the term *aphantasia* originally referred to the absence of visual imagery, researchers and lived experience reports have since clarified that it often extends into other sensory modalities. This is what we now call *multisensory aphantasia*, the absence of mental imagery across multiple, or even all, sensory channels.

Clients with multisensory aphantasia may be unable to:

- Hear sounds in their mind (auditory imagery)
- Recreate physical sensations (kinaesthetic imagery)
- Imagine tastes, smells, or tactile sensations
- Rehearse actions mentally (motor imagery)

In therapy, this becomes significant. A client with multisensory aphantasia may not be able to hear their own internal voice, imagine the sound of a loved one's laughter, or picture themselves succeeding at a future goal. They may not be able to engage in sensory recall or re-live an experience with any emotional or bodily resonance.

What this means is that many standard therapeutic tools, guided visualisation, sensory grounding, somatic memory work, fall flat. Not due to resistance or lack of engagement, but because the internal resources these techniques rely on are simply not available.

This creates a need for externalisation, creative metaphor, and a profound shift in how we conceptualise the therapeutic process.

The spectrum of imagery vividness: aphantasia to hyperphantasia

Aphantasia doesn't exist in isolation. It is part of a wider spectrum of imagery vividness, from complete absence to exceptionally vivid mental imagery. At one end of the spectrum is aphantasia, the total lack of voluntary mental imagery. At the other end is hyperphantasia, where mental images are so vivid they can be difficult to distinguish from real perception.

Between these extremes are varying degrees of imagery strength:

- Aphantasia: no voluntary mental imagery
- Hypophantasia: limited or faint mental imagery
- Phantasia: average mental imagery
- Hyperphantasia: extremely vivid, often lifelike imagery

Whilst there are a growing number of research papers relating to aphantasia, there are still wide differences between the prevalence numbers. Figures range from 0.89% of the population having global aphantasia (all senses) to between 3.9% and 5% for visual imagery alone. Professor Adam Zeman, whose research coined the name aphantasia, has said that these figures rise to between 5% and 10% with more generous criteria for inclusion.

This means that potentially 10% of your clients may be working from a much less visually vivid internal landscape than average. If we just used 5% as our prevalence figure, at the time of writing, this equates to roughly 410 million people worldwide who can't visualise. Many of them are already in your therapy room.

Aphantasia can be congenital, in that people are born with it, or acquired because of brain damage/trauma.

Understanding this spectrum matters because therapy often presumes an average or above-average capacity for visualisation. Yet many clients, particularly those with aphantasia or hypophantasia, may struggle with techniques that assume internal visual representation, even if they don't disclose this.

Neurological research findings

Scientific research into aphantasia is still relatively young, but what we know so far reveals meaningful neurological distinctions between individuals with aphantasia and those with typical or heightened imagery.

One of the most widely cited studies comes from Professor Adam Zeman and colleagues at the University of Exeter. Using brain scans, researchers compared people who can't visualise with those who can. When asked to imagine faces or places, the brains of people who can visualise 'lit up' in the areas responsible for creating mental pictures. People with aphantasia showed little or no activity in these same areas.

Other studies looked at eye movements and pupil changes. People who can visualise show unconscious pupil responses when they imagine bright or dark scenes. People with aphantasia, however, don't. This lends itself to a potential diagnostic tool.

Importantly, these neurological markers suggest that aphantasia isn't about unwillingness or psychological avoidance. Unless it's acquired, it isn't a result of trauma, repression, or resistance. It is a cognitive variation that changes how a person engages with mental imagery and, by extension, with many of the techniques therapy assumes they can use.

Common language and behaviour patterns in clients with aphantasia

In the therapy room, clients with aphantasia often reveal their inner experience through subtle linguistic cues and behavioural patterns. These signs are frequently overlooked, particularly when therapists are unaware of the difference, but once you know what to listen for, the signals become easier to spot.

Clients may speak in short, factual sentences rather than vivid, descriptive narratives. Their storytelling may lack sensory detail or emotional colour. For example, instead of saying, "I remember feeling the icy wind against my face as I stood there," they might say, "It was cold." The facts are there, but the felt experience is missing.

Common phrases include:

- "It's just blank when I try to picture it."
- "I don't really remember what it looked like."
- "I know it happened, but I can't see it."
- "I'm not sure how I felt."

They might struggle to describe internal sensations or to 'tap into' emotions through imagination or imagery. Instead, they may excel in analysis, logic, or verbal processing. These clients are often intelligent, self-aware, and motivated, but something in therapy never quite clicks.

Noticing this pattern can be the first step towards asking the kind of questions that opens the door to greater understanding.

Common myths and misunderstandings

Even as awareness of aphantasia begins to grow, misconceptions persist, often subtly woven into everyday language, cultural assumptions, and therapeutic training. For therapists, it is essential to untangle these myths, not only for the sake of clinical accuracy but to avoid inadvertently pathologising or dismissing a client's experience.

Myth 1: Aphantasia is just a lack of imagination

One of the most pervasive misconceptions is that people with aphantasia lack imagination, creativity, or emotional depth. This couldn't be further from the truth. Imagination isn't synonymous with imagery. A person can ideate, create, and invent without forming pictures in their mind. Many writers, scientists, and artists with aphantasia describe having vivid internal landscapes, just not in visual or sensory form.

Myth 2: Aphantasia is caused by trauma or psychological defence.

While imagery suppression can occur in trauma-related dissociation, aphantasia isn't a trauma response. Neurological research indicates it is a cognitive trait, not a defensive adaptation. Mistaking aphantasia for emotional avoidance can lead to misguided interventions that unintentionally invalidate the client's truth.

Myth 3: People with aphantasia just need practice visualising.

This belief is both inaccurate and harmful. Aphantasia isn't a skill deficit. It isn't something that can be corrected through repetition or guided exercises. Clients are often told to "try harder" or "go with whatever comes," which only deepens their sense of alienation when nothing comes at all.

Myth 4: You can't do therapy without visualisation.

Many effective therapeutic modalities don't rely on imagery. While approaches like IFS, EMDR, or guided visualisation may be popular, they are not the only routes to healing. With creativity and attunement, therapy can be profoundly effective using external tools, verbal reflection, metaphor, and somatic awareness.

Myth 5: If a client doesn't report images, they're not trying or engaging.

Clients with aphantasia often feel they are "doing therapy wrong." Some will even fabricate imagery to avoid disappointing their therapist. What looks like disengagement is survival. It is the result of trying to meet the expectations of a therapeutic model that doesn't recognise their cognitive difference.

Myth 6: Aphantasia is always total.

Imagery vividness exists on a spectrum, and many people fall somewhere between typical imagery and complete absence. A client may be able to visualise in some contexts but not others. They may experience flashes of imagery only in dreams, or visual fragments that lack clarity. These nuances are important, and rigid categories can miss the individual variation that exists.

How aphantasia can be masked in therapy

One of the reasons aphantasia remains largely invisible is because many clients, especially those with no prior knowledge of the difference, unknowingly mask it. Before I knew about aphantasia, I didn't know that I wasn't visualising.

If you had asked me to picture my inner child I might have described a child, from a place of knowing what one is. I just wouldn't have been 'seeing' my inner child or connecting to her. Masking can also become a form of self-protection, shaped by a desire to meet expectations, maintain rapport, and avoid the discomfort of being misunderstood.

Clients assume everyone is like them

In the absence of shared language or education, many people with aphantasia grow up believing that everyone experiences the world the way they do. If they've never had mental pictures, they assume no one does. Like me, when asked to visualise something, they might interpret it metaphorically: "Think about a beach," becomes "Think about what you know about beaches. List all those things." The literal absence of imagery isn't even recognised as a difference.

As a result, the client doesn't say, *"I can't see anything."* They say, *"I guess it's sunny, there are waves,"* drawing from knowledge of what a beach is, rather than internal experience. To the therapist, it can appear as if the intervention is working.

Clients don't want to disappoint

Therapy often carries an unspoken dynamic of "doing it right." Clients want to meet the expectations of the process and avoid conflict or awkwardness. So, when a technique is introduced that doesn't resonate, such as imagining an inner child or visualising a safe place, they may feel pressured to participate in ways that aren't authentic.

They may:

- Use vague or generic imagery.

- Echo the therapist's suggestions.
- Invent responses that fit the exercise.
- Nod along while feeling increasingly disconnected.

This is accommodation, not manipulation. The client is trying to fit into a model that feels implicitly required, often without fully understanding why it doesn't feel natural.

Masking as compliance

Compliance is one of the most misleading signals in therapy. A client may appear engaged, offer coherent reflections, and complete homework tasks, yet still feel confused, unseen, or emotionally flat. When those clients later disengage, it may be misinterpreted as loss of motivation or lack of readiness.

The truth is that the disconnection was there all along. It simply wasn't recognised, understood or named.

The cost of masking

When a client repeatedly tries to engage in exercises that feel hollow or meaningless, they may begin to internalise that failure. Thoughts like:

- *"I must not be trying hard enough."*
- *"Maybe I'm not open to change."*
- *"Something must be wrong with me."*

This quiet erosion of self-trust can be profoundly damaging. The client may leave therapy feeling more confused, ashamed, or isolated than when they arrived.

When the therapist doesn't know either

Even when a therapist is open-minded and client-centred, the absence of knowledge about aphantasia can make it difficult to recognise what's happening. Most training doesn't include awareness of this difference, so subtle signs are often misread, leaving clients silently wondering why therapy doesn't seem to work for them.

Therapeutic implications and what to do next

The goal of this chapter isn't to suggest that therapy has failed clients with aphantasia, but to highlight a gap in awareness and to encourage clinicians to become curious about the diversity of minds that enter their consulting rooms.

Therapists are not expected to be experts in every form of neurodivergence, but you are expected to listen, to respond, and to adapt. That begins with asking better questions and letting go of rigid assumptions.

If you've recognised some of your clients in this chapter, here are a few practical starting points:

- Stay open: If a client tells you they can't picture, sense, or recall something internally, believe them. Don't assume it's resistance.
- Adjust your language: Replace "visualise" with "think about" or "recall as best you can." Focus on verbal or behavioural responses.
- Normalise the difference: Acknowledge that minds work differently. Let clients know they're not alone or broken.

- Use external tools: Diagrams, timelines, object metaphors, and written reflections often work better than imaginative exercises.

These small shifts can transform the therapy experience. They move the process from exclusion to inclusion, from assumed universality to genuine attunement.

You don't need to master aphantasia to support someone who has it, but you do need to know it exists. To recognise that when someone says, "I can't picture it," they might not be asking for help, they might be offering you the key to understanding them.

In the next chapters, we'll explore related cognitive differences, how they intersect with aphantasia and why they matter. For now, remember this:

Aphantasia isn't a limitation but a difference, and your willingness to adapt may be the turning point a client never knew they needed.

Asking the right questions: clues and curiosity in practice

You don't need to diagnose aphantasia, in fact, you shouldn't as that's not your role. What you can do, and what will make the greatest difference, is ask questions that reveal how your client's mind works.

Be a practitioner who is curious rather than assuming, responsive rather than directive.

Here are some ways to open that curiosity.

Gentle inquiry

Early in the therapeutic relationship, or whenever a client appears to disengage from an experiential exercise, it can be helpful to ask:

- *"When I invite you to imagine something, what happens inside your mind?"*
- *"Do you tend to think in pictures, sounds, words, or something else?"*
- *"When you remember a moment from the past, is it more like a picture, a feeling, a thought, or something else entirely?"*

These questions are neutral, open-ended, and respectful, with nothing invasive about them. They invite the client to reflect on their own inner experience without imposing expectations.

Noticing the gaps

Sometimes, aphantasia reveals itself not through what is said, but what is missing. A client may tell a detailed story but include no sensory or emotional language. They may recount life events with flat affect, using factual statements with no visual or emotional detail.

You might gently say:

- *"As you're describing that, I notice there's not a lot of imagery or emotional tone. Does that reflect how you experience it internally?"*

Or:

- *"Is it okay if I ask, when you say you remember that, are you seeing it in your mind or just recalling the facts?"*

Even if the client doesn't know the term aphantasia, they might say something like, *"I don't really see it, I just know it happened."* That's your sign to adapt.

The role of curiosity in inclusivity

Curiosity is at the heart of inclusive practice. It allows you to see beyond surface behaviours, beyond technique-based frameworks, and into the lived reality of the person in front of you.

When you ask thoughtful questions about a client's internal experience, you send a powerful message:

"I want to know how things work for you, not how they're supposed to work for everyone."

What not to do: common pitfalls and missteps

Even the most compassionate therapist can unintentionally reinforce a client's sense of failure if the approach isn't adapted for their cognitive experience. Many clients with aphantasia describe therapy as something they thought they were "failing at" because the tools didn't fit.

Avoiding these common missteps can prevent unnecessary harm and open the door to deeper connection.

1. Don't gently push "just try" techniques

When a client says, *"I can't picture it,"* the most well-meaning response often sounds like:

- *"That's okay, just go with whatever comes."*
- *"Even if it's vague, just imagine something."*
- *"Give it a try anyway, there's no wrong way."*

For someone with aphantasia, there is no way. These responses unintentionally suggest that the client isn't trying hard enough or that the technique would work if they were more open. Over time, this can chip away at their trust in both you and them.

Instead, acknowledge what they've said:

- *"Thanks for letting me know. Let's find another way."*
- *"You don't need to visualise. We can work differently."*

2. Don't interpret difficulty as resistance

Therapists are trained to explore blocks and defences. When a client doesn't respond to visualisation, memory work, or emotion-focused techniques, the reflexive response is often to look for what's being defended or avoided.

This isn't always wrong, but it can become a default explanation that misses something crucial: the client might not be avoiding at all, they may simply be unable to do what's being asked of them.

Treating cognitive differences as emotional resistance can feel invalidating and confusing to the client. They may start to internalise the belief that they are emotionally detached, psychologically blocked, or 'not ready for the work', when in fact, they are just neurologically different.

3. Don't assume they know their difference

Many clients don't know what aphantasia is and may have never questioned how their mind works. They've lived with a blank mind's eye their whole life and assumed everyone else experienced the same.

So, when they say, *"I don't know,"* or *"Nothing's coming up,"* they're describing their actual experience, without the language to name it.

Rather than assuming disengagement, treat these moments as an opportunity for inquiry. Your curiosity could be the first time someone has ever invited them to explore the way their mind works.

4. Don't Label Them as "Not Suited to Therapy"

Perhaps most damaging of all is the subtle conclusion some therapists reach when repeated attempts to use common tools fall flat: *"Maybe this client just isn't suited to this kind of work."*

This belief might never be voiced, but it shows up in how the sessions feel. Less energy, fewer interventions, an unspoken sense of detachment.

Clients feel this.

From my own experience, I know that I 'checked out' during sessions and, whilst unintentional, it felt to me like my therapist had done that too.

Therapy that doesn't help is only part of the danger. The greater harm is that the client leaves believing they can't be helped, and that sense of being "too complicated," "too difficult," or "too broken" can follow them for years.

A way forward: adaptation as attunement

The good news is that supporting clients with aphantasia doesn't require a complete overhaul of your practice.

Adaptation, in this context, means attunement, the core of therapeutic presence. It never means lowering the bar or simplifying the work.

You already know how to adapt because you already do it. When a client is dysregulated, you slow your pace. When they avoid eye contact, you soften your gaze. When they need structure, you offer containment. Adapting to aphantasia is no different. It begins with noticing and responding to the client in front of you, rather than the one you imagined.

Here are a few starting points.

Ask openly about cognitive experience

Early in your work together, or when something isn't landing, you might ask:

"When I use words like 'visualise,' does an image actually come up for you, or is it more abstract, a 'knowing'?"

This question is non-invasive, respectful, and curiosity driven. It invites exploration, rather than explanation.

Replace imagery with externalisation

If the client can't conjure an inner image, give them something tangible. You might try:

- Drawing a timeline rather than visualising a life path
- Using objects or cards to represent parts, feelings, or memories
- Writing lists or using metaphors in dialogue rather than imagination
- Asking for factual recall rather than emotional re-experiencing

External tools allow clients with aphantasia to show you what's happening in their world, without relying on an inner canvas they don't have.

Support emotional exploration without visual triggers

Clients with aphantasia may struggle to connect with emotions through visual prompts or sensory recall. Instead:

- Use bodily language, if accessible: "Where do you feel that in your body?" (though this may also be flat if interoception is reduced)
- Anchor emotions in present-day events or patterns rather than memories
- Reflect back the emotional tone of their words, voice, or posture to help them build emotional awareness

Not all clients will be able to name or feel their emotions clearly, but your calm, steady presence helps build safety to explore even the faintest signals.

Let them lead

If you're not sure how your client processes internally, ask:

- *"What kind of things help you make sense of what's happening?"*
- *"When you think about change, what feels useful for you?"*
- *"Is it helpful for you when I ask you to imagine things, or is there another way you'd prefer to explore this?"*

Clients with aphantasia often feel immense relief when given permission to work differently. It validates not just their preference, but their experience of self.

Be transparent about your learning

If you're new to this area, you don't need to pretend otherwise. In fact, sharing that you're learning about aphantasia and related differences can be deeply reassuring for clients who have felt misunderstood or dismissed.

Try saying:

- *"This might sound like a strange question, but have you ever heard of aphantasia?"*
- *"Some people don't visualise or hear an inner voice. I'm learning more about this and trying to be mindful of it in our work."*
- *"Let me know if something I offer doesn't land; there might be another way that works better for you."*

This simple honesty models humility and openness and helps build trust that is so often lost when clients feel misinterpreted.

Closing thoughts: beyond awareness, towards inclusion

Understanding aphantasia expands your lens rather than adding another label to your clinical vocabulary. It's about recognising that, for all the complexity we explore in therapy, trauma, attachment, identity, emotion, there is a foundational layer we often overlook: how the mind works.

Aphantasia, and its multisensory variations, are not disorders. These are differences, not pathologies, and they intersect with therapy at almost every point: from assessment to technique, and from rapport-building to emotional processing. When we don't know they exist, we risk misreading silence as avoidance, factual speech as disconnection, and cognitive flatness as emotional repression.

The invitation in this chapter, and this book, isn't to become an expert in every form of neurodivergence. It is just to stay curious. To listen differently. To approach the unknown with humility and care.

When a client tells you they can't picture something, believe them. When they struggle to name feelings or recall childhood experiences, consider that the barrier may be cognitive, not emotional. When traditional tools don't seem to land, don't push harder, pivot.

You already have the skills. You already have the relational capacity. What this work asks of you is awareness, and the courage to acknowledge that even the most well-established methods may not work for every mind.

In the chapters to come, we will explore more of these differences, how they interact, how they're experienced, and how they shape the therapy room in ways we're only just beginning to understand.

For now, let this chapter be a marker.

A starting point.

A gentle turning of your gaze towards what has, for too long, gone unseen.

Reflective practice

Set aside ten to fifteen minutes to sit with the following questions. You may wish to journal your responses, discuss them in supervision, or use them as prompts for your own professional development planning.

1. *Have you ever had a client who seemed emotionally flat, disconnected from memory, or vague in response to imagery-based work? What were your working assumptions about that client's process?*
2. *How would you now revisit that case considering what you know about aphantasia? Would you try a different approach? Ask different questions?*
3. *What is your own relationship with internal imagery? Are you a highly visual thinker? How might that shape your assumptions about others?*
4. *Consider the language you use in your practice. How often do you say things like "picture this," "imagine," or "see what comes up"? Could some of that language be softened or expanded?*
5. *Small shifts make a big difference. Write down one change you will make in your next assessment or session to account for cognitive difference.*

Chapter 4

SDAM: a life without memories

There's a moment in many therapy sessions where the past is meant to rise to the surface. A therapist leans forward gently and says something like, "Can you take yourself back there?" Or "What was happening in your body at the time?" Or perhaps, "What do you see when you think of that day?"

In that moment, the client is expected to scan their mind, and retrieve not just facts, but feelings, images, sensory echoes. An experience that plays like a scene in a film, textured with emotion and lived perspective.

For clients with Severely Deficient Autobiographical Memory (SDAM), that moment lands differently.

Instead of a vivid scene, there is nothing. Instead of emotion, there is information, or a story of a memory. Instead of a vivid internal world, there is a logical list, who was there, what happened, and in what order, but none of the feeling. The memory might be known but not re-experienced. It might be understood but not re-lived. Sometimes there is no memory at all.

This gap between what therapy expects and what the client can access creates a subtle but powerful rupture. The client might say something like, "I remember being there, but I don't feel it," or "I know it happened, but it's like someone told me the story, it doesn't feel like it happened to me."

Therapists, trained to interpret emotional disconnection through lenses of trauma or defence, might gently suggest that the client is avoiding something. That they're dissociating. That there is more beneath the surface, waiting to emerge.

What if there's not? What if the client is already offering the full extent of their recall?

What if the issue isn't avoidance at all, but a different cognitive structure entirely?

For those with SDAM, this is simply the baseline. There is no temporary block to wait out and no protective mechanism to work through. Their mind doesn't reach into the past to re-live emotion or remember the event. It retrieves facts, like flipping through a document rather than opening a film. The richness of emotional memory, the visceral connection that so many therapeutic approaches rely on, is simply absent.

Yet until recently, this difference has remained largely invisible in therapy. It is rarely named, often misinterpreted, and even more often missed entirely.

The result.

Clients and therapists can feel stuck, and therapy loses its thread, not because the work is impossible, but because the starting point was misunderstood.

In the sections that follow, we'll unpack what SDAM really is, how it differs from other forms of memory difficulty, and how therapy can adapt to support clients who experience life without the ability to re-live their past.

What is SDAM? A clinical introduction

Severely Deficient Autobiographical Memory (SDAM) is a term first introduced by Dr Brian Levine and his research team at the Rotman Research Institute in 2015. The difference refers to the inability to mentally re-experience past personal events. In simpler terms, individuals with SDAM can remember the facts of their life, but not the feelings.

They might know what happened, but they can't *re-live* it.

This isn't the same as poor memory. In fact, people with SDAM often have excellent recall of dates, timelines, and historical information about their lives. They can tell you that they went to primary school in Yorkshire, that their grandfather died in 2003, that they had a stressful week at work in March, but they can't feel any of those events internally. They can't conjure images, re-access emotions, or replay scenes in their mind.

It is, fundamentally, a difference in *episodic memory*, not in intelligence or general knowledge.

Episodic memory is the part of long-term memory that allows us to recall specific personal experiences, complete with the associated context and emotional tone. It's what lets someone remember not just what happened on their wedding day, but how it felt to walk down the aisle. It's what brings the tears when recalling a moment of loss, or the warmth when thinking about a favourite childhood memory.

For people with SDAM, this richness is absent. They have semantic memories, the memory of facts, general knowledge and concepts, but very limited or no episodic or life memories.

The effect is a kind of internal flatness, not emotionally numb, not repressed, but simply unable to travel back in time through memory. For many, the emotional tone of past events isn't retrievable, not even with prompting; for some, a feeling or bodily trace survives even when everything around it is gone.

Nearly all of the photographs of me on my wedding day show me beaming from ear to ear and I remember that my cheeks had started to hurt because I was smiling so much. I must have been happy, but I have no memory of that happiness, it's just something obvious to me because the photographs show me that.

Crucially, SDAM isn't a disorder, and it isn't classified in the DSM or ICD. It is a cognitive variation, much like aphantasia. Also, much like aphantasia, it isn't well known, even among clinicians, which is why many clients with SDAM go undiagnosed or mislabelled for years.

In fact, much of what makes SDAM difficult in therapy isn't the experience itself, but the lack of awareness around it. When therapists assume that emotional memory is universally accessible, the absence of it is framed as pathology, avoidance, trauma response, or emotional resistance.

It creates a therapeutic environment in which clients feel unseen or judged for something that isn't within their control and it leads to a mismatch in expectations, outcomes, and relational connection.

Understanding SDAM, therefore, isn't about pathologising a difference but about recognising it as a legitimate variation in human experience and adapting therapy accordingly.

The strands of re-living

Brian Levine and his colleagues, who named SDAM in 2015, describe it as a lifelong inability to vividly relive or re-experience personal events. That definition rests on Endel Tulving's distinction between episodic and semantic memory. Episodic memory is the system that lets a person travel back into subjective time and stand inside a moment again. Semantic memory holds the facts about our lives. In SDAM, the semantic record survives while the episodic return does not.

What the definition doesn't spell out, and what matters enormously in the therapy room, is that re-living is not one single experience. It has strands. There is the visual scene, the narrative thread of who was there and what unfolded, the emotional tone of the moment, and the bodily sense that accompanied it. For most people these strands arrive woven together in one vivid replay, which is why therapy has tended to treat them as one thing.

In SDAM, the episodic machinery that binds and replays those strands is what's affected. Emotional memory, though, is supported partly by separate systems in the brain, which helps to explain why the emotional strand doesn't behave identically for everyone who has SDAM.

For many people with SDAM, myself included, every strand is out of reach. Memories are factual and emotionally flat. There is no stepping back into the moment, no re-feeling of what was felt then, and no way of generating that feeling now. The past reads like a record written by someone else. In my conversations with people who share this difference, and across the community discussions I follow, this appears to be the most commonly described experience, and it is the profile this chapter explores in depth, because it is the one therapy most often misreads. I should also name my own lens here: I live with alexithymia alongside SDAM, and so do many of the people drawn to my work, which may shape both what I hear and how I interpret it. No research has yet mapped how common each profile is.

Since publishing the first edition of this book, I've heard from a handful of people with SDAM who describe something different. Some retain clear factual knowledge of what they felt at the time, they know they felt ashamed, or afraid, or furious, and in knowing it, they can generate that feeling in the present. A client might carry the burn of a humiliation from decades ago, whilst only having the factual details of what happened or a retelling of the story of the event. There may be more than one route to that feeling. It may be a preserved trace of the original emotion. It may be generated afresh from the factual knowledge of what was felt. It may even be a new emotion entirely, arriving with hindsight as the person looks back at the event through who they are now, and I've noticed that a feeling can arrive or shift in the very act of retelling. Whether the feeling is retrieved from the past or created in the present is almost impossible to settle from the inside, and for our purposes how it is generated barely matters. What matters is the shape it leaves in the room.

For others, even the factual record is thin. The feeling arrives vivid and specific while the details a therapist might reach for, who was there, what was said, how the day ended, are largely missing in any form.

That shape carries its own clinical risk. A therapist who hears strong, specific emotion will reasonably assume the client can step back inside the moment it belongs to, and will ask exactly the questions this client cannot answer. Can you stay with that image? Take yourself back there, what do you notice? How did it feel as it was happening? For this client there is no moment to step back into, only the feeling and the factual account, and where the factual record is also thin, even questions of context meet the same wall. Without an understanding of SDAM, those answers can be misread as evasion, as fragmentation, or as resistance. This is the mirror image of the misreading the rest of this chapter describes, and it connects with something we will return to later in this chapter, when we look at SDAM and trauma: distress that cannot be pictured or narrated does not disappear, and often arrives in the body instead.

Whichever profile is sitting opposite you, the adaptation is the same, and it runs through this whole book. Ask rather than assume, and start from what is present. For one client, what is present will be facts, patterns and meaning. For another, it will be a feeling with no story attached. Both are workable, once they are recognised for what they are.

Neuroscience of memory and SDAM

To understand SDAM more deeply, we need to take a brief detour into how memory works in the brain.

Autobiographical memory isn't stored in one location. Instead, it relies on a network of brain regions that integrate different elements of experience, what happened, where it happened, how it felt, and what it meant. These include:

- The hippocampus, which plays a central role in forming new episodic memories.
- The medial prefrontal cortex, which helps us assign meaning and personal relevance.
- The amygdala, which adds emotional weight to experiences.
- The posterior cingulate cortex, which contributes to the feeling of self over time.

Together, these regions enable us to mentally "time travel", to step into our memories and re-live them, emotionally and sensorily. This is the heart of what most people think of as memory: a vivid, internal replay.

In individuals with SDAM, research has shown that this network appears to function differently.

A 2016 neuroimaging study by Palombo et al. revealed that people with SDAM tend to have smaller-than-average hippocampal volumes, particularly in the region linked to episodic memory. This doesn't mean the hippocampus is damaged or non-functional, but it does suggest a neurological basis for the difficulty in re-experiencing past events.

Other studies have found that, when asked to recall personal memories, people with SDAM show reduced activation in the core autobiographical memory network. Their brains don't "light up" in the same way, especially in areas associated with vivid visual imagery and emotional recall.

Interestingly, despite this difference, semantic memory areas remain intact or even stronger. This aligns with lived experience reports and individuals with SDAM tend to have excellent factual memory, often recalling dates, timelines, and contextual details with high accuracy, but not the accompanying feeling.

In short, it's not that SDAM clients aren't *trying* to recall emotional content. Their brains simply don't retrieve personal experiences in the same way. It's a structural and functional variation, not a deficit in effort, willingness, or emotional availability.

This is a vital reframe for therapy.

When a client with SDAM can't "go back" into a memory, it's not that they are avoiding or resisting. It's that the memory, as therapists commonly conceptualise it, doesn't exist in their mind in that form. There is no internal movie to replay.

Recognising this opens the door to profound compassion and adaptation. Instead of pushing the client to remember emotionally, we can shift the work to meaning, values, or present-focused observation. We can do so knowing that the client is working with a different neurological map rather than working against us.

Why therapists often misread SDAM

When therapy misreads SDAM: assumptions, misinterpretations, and missed cues

In most therapeutic models, emotional recall is a cornerstone of insight and healing. Therapists are trained to listen not just for content, but for emotional resonance and those subtle cues that connect past experience with present pain. When those cues are absent or muted, the default interpretations are familiar: trauma repression, emotional avoidance, dissociation, or relational resistance.

What if the absence of emotional re-living isn't a defence mechanism? What if it is simply the way some minds function?

Clients with SDAM might know *what* happened in their past, but not *how* it felt. They might describe a significant event with accuracy and clarity but without the effect that therapists expect. They could speak of grief, fear, or even abuse in a matter-of-fact tone, and to the untrained ear, that flatness may sound like shutdown.

Here are a few of the most common ways SDAM is misunderstood in the therapy room:

1. They're avoiding the work.

A therapist introduces memory work or inner child exercises. The client says they don't remember much, or they're unsure how they felt at the time. The therapist interprets this as avoidance, encouraging the client to "stay with it" or "go deeper."

For the SDAM client, there is no 'deeper' to go. What may look like resistance is often simply the edge of their cognitive experience.

2. They're repressing something

The emotional flatness of SDAM is often mistaken for psychological repression. Therapists may assume the client has cut off access to memory as a protective response to trauma.

While this may be true for some, SDAM presents a different picture. These clients may have excellent factual recall, listing dates, names, and sequences of events. What many of them lack is the felt sense of memories. Often there is no visceral trace and no emotional echo. The client is describing absence, not avoidance.

3. They're not engaging

When clients with SDAM appear analytical or overly cognitive, therapists may worry that the work isn't landing. They may try to bypass the client's logical thinking to get to "the heart" of the matter.

For SDAM clients, logic is the heart of the matter. Insight, pattern recognition, and meaning-making are the doorway in, and there is nothing superficial about that route. Asking them to bypass this is asking them to abandon the very tools they use to understand themselves.

The trap of emotional expectation

Therapists often use emotion as a compass. We look for tears, affect shifts, and bodily reactions. When these are missing, we get curious, but sometimes in the wrong direction. We ask, "What's being defended?" instead of "What's possible in a mind like this?"

It's an innocent mistake, but a costly one. When emotional reactivity is treated as the only evidence of therapeutic progress, clients with SDAM are pathologised for being who they are.

Small Comments, Big Consequences

Sometimes, misunderstandings are subtle. A therapist might gently say, "I wonder if you're keeping something at bay," or "Maybe it's hard to go there right now." These are offered with care, but they can seed doubt in the client's mind.

They may begin to believe that they're not ready, not capable, or not emotionally literate. They may start to feel ashamed of their way of remembering, and eventually, they may disengage, not because they didn't care, but because they didn't feel safe to be honest.

Emma's story

Emma, a 36-year-old solicitor, came to therapy after a close friend's sudden death. She described feeling "completely thrown" by the grief, yet also strangely disconnected from it. "It's like I know she's gone," she said in her initial session, "but I don't feel it unless I see the flowers on her grave."

Emma was well-spoken, thoughtful, and clearly motivated to understand her emotional state. She told her therapist that she hadn't cried and couldn't seem to connect with any strong emotions when thinking about the loss. "It's like she's totally absent from my mind. I can't see her face in my mind and I'm struggling to remember the things we did together. She's just gone"

Using an integrative relational approach, Emma was invited to revisit her last conversation with her friend. "See if you can go back into that moment. What do you see, feel, hear?"

Emma paused, then shrugged gently. "I know where we were. I think I know some of the things we talked about. It's all a bit vague really. Shouldn't I be feeling something? No wonder people think I've got a heart of stone"

Her therapist gently encouraged her to stay with it. "Sometimes the feeling comes with a little time. Let's just breathe and give it space."

Nothing came. Emma sat in silence, trying hard to do what was being asked, but unable to access the emotional tone her therapist seemed to expect. After a few more sessions like this, she began to question herself. "Maybe I'm not ready. Maybe I'm frozen," she said.

In supervision, her therapist noted the absence of effect and explored the idea of unresolved trauma or repressed emotion. Emma, meanwhile, quietly Googled phrases like "why can't I remember my past?" and eventually found a blog post describing SDAM. It was like it had been written about her.

With this insight, she brought the idea to her therapist. "I think I might have this thing called Severely Deficient Autobiographical Memory. It sounds like me." Her therapist listened with curiosity, did her own reading between sessions, and together they began to adapt the work.

They stopped trying to re-live the past and instead, they explored what the loss meant to Emma now. They used metaphor, values, and present-day responses to anchor their work. Emma began journaling, not about feelings from the past, but about how she noticed grief showing up in her body in the here and now. She used rating scales, practical tracking, and external tools to help build awareness. She wrote about the stories of their friendship.

Over time, Emma came to understand that she wasn't disconnected from her emotions. She simply didn't experience her memories in the same way others did, and that didn't make her incapable of healing. It just meant she needed a different path. Emma's experience reflects the flat, factual profile; as we saw earlier, the emotional strand behaves differently for some.

Why this matters

When therapists misread SDAM as avoidance, disconnection, or repression, the entire foundation of the therapeutic relationship becomes shaky with the client feeling misunderstood and the therapist starts to question the client's engagement. Eventually, both are working at cross-purposes.

This isn't a failure of care. Most therapy models are built on the assumption that memory includes feeling. That the past isn't just remembered but re-lived. When that assumption goes unchallenged, SDAM clients are left out of the model and often out of the healing process.

Recognising SDAM in the therapy room

Severely Deficient Autobiographical Memory is still a relatively unknown difference. It isn't widely discussed in counselling training, rarely mentioned in supervision, and almost never included in the differential thinking around therapeutic resistance. Yet it may be quietly shaping the experiences of many clients who leave therapy feeling misunderstood.

So how can therapists begin to recognise SDAM in practice?

The signs are subtle, but they often emerge in how clients respond to questions about their past and in the texture of their storytelling. Here are some cues that may indicate a client has SDAM:

1. Flat or detached emotional descriptions

Clients with SDAM may talk about significant life events, losses, achievements, and traumas, in a tone that sounds surprisingly neutral. They may say things like:

- "I know it was a hard time, but I can't remember feeling upset."
- "It's strange, I know I loved him, but I don't feel anything now."
- "It's just feels like a story I tell myself."

Rather than indicating emotional detachment or suppression, these statements may reflect the client's genuine lack of access to felt memory.

2. Factual storytelling

Their recall of personal events often sounds more like a timeline than a vivid narrative. There is usually little in the way of sensory detail, emotional colour, or reflective meaning unless prompted to interpret cognitively.

3. Struggling with standard memory prompts

When invited to "go back to that moment" or "picture yourself in that situation," they may look confused or say:

- "I don't remember anything about it, I just know it happened"
- "I can tell you what happened, but I can't see it."
- "I know that it was a big moment, but I don't feel connected to it."

Each of these is an accurate description of how the client's memory works rather than an evasion.

4. Difficulty connecting emotionally to the past

Clients with SDAM may have no difficulty accessing current feelings and can tell you that they're anxious, sad, frustrated, or stuck, but when you ask how those feelings relate to past experiences, they may say they don't know, or they'll make logical guesses without emotional certainty. They may say:

- "I think that probably affected me, but I'm not sure how."

- "I know it was important, but I don't have strong feelings about it."

5. Repeated self-doubt or apologising

Therapeutic culture prizes emotional insight and memory-based exploration, so clients with SDAM can begin to feel as though they're failing the process. They may apologise for "not doing it right," express concerns that they're too analytical or "too in their head," or question whether they're making progress.

This self-doubt is often a reaction to implicit expectations. They can sense that something isn't landing in the way the therapist had hoped, and without an explanation, they internalise it as a personal shortcoming.

By learning to recognise these signs, therapists can begin to differentiate between cognitive differences and psychological defence. Recognising SDAM requires a shift in clinical reasoning from interpreting through familiar emotional frameworks to developing curiosity about unseen cognitive architecture.

SDAM isn't a block to overcome, but a different path entirely.

Reframing the role of memory in therapy

When therapists begin to understand SDAM not as a psychological defence but as a cognitive difference, a subtle but powerful shift becomes possible. Instead of pushing for emotional recollection, therapy can move towards reflective meaning-making, pattern awareness, and values-based exploration.

This doesn't mean abandoning the past altogether but re-evaluating how we work with it.

From emotional re-living to cognitive reflection

Traditional approaches often guide clients back into emotionally charged memories to 're-process' experiences. This may involve revisiting a difficult childhood event, working with sensory recall, or attempting to access the "inner child." These can be incredibly powerful tools when the client has access to that level of inner experience.

For clients with SDAM, nothing is blocking that kind of depth. It simply doesn't exist in the form you might expect. Insight doesn't have to come from emotional re-living, though. It can come from reflecting on what the client has learned, how patterns have formed, and what choices they now wish to make moving forward.

Instead of asking "How did it feel?"

You might ask "What sense have you made of that experience?" or "What did you take away from that moment that still affects you now?" or "How has that situation shaped your current values or beliefs?"

These types of questions honour the client's strengths, logic, self-observation, and conceptual thinking, without pathologising what's absent.

Memory as narrative, not footage

Therapists can support SDAM clients by treating memory not as emotional footage to be replayed, but as a narrative thread to be examined. Clients may not recall how it felt to be left out at school, but they might know that they learned to expect exclusion. That belief, not the event itself, becomes the work.

In this way, therapy becomes less about retrieving a past feeling and more about updating the client's internal map, correcting distortions, questioning assumptions, and building agency in the present.

Therapeutic alliance as emotional anchor

In SDAM-informed therapy, the emotional depth may not come from the client's memory, but from the relationship. When the therapist listens without pressuring, believes without probing, and adapts without judgement, a profound sense of safety is created.

For many clients with SDAM, this relational attunement may be the most emotionally impactful part of therapy. It's where the emotional tone resides, not in the client's memory, but in the therapist's responsiveness.

Signs you might be working with a client with SDAM

Clients with SDAM often go undetected in therapy, not because their needs are hidden, but because the signs are easy to misread. Unless a therapist is specifically looking for indicators of autobiographical memory difference, it is common to interpret these clients through a more familiar lens of resistance, emotional avoidance, detachment, or intellectualisation.

Let's explore some of the clues that may point to SDAM in practice.

1. Their memory sounds like a report

Clients with SDAM tend to describe life events in the style of a timeline, spreadsheet, or bullet-point summary. They may say:

- "It happened in 1997. I was in Year 9. It was just after my cousin's wedding."
- "I know I was upset, but I don't remember feeling anything in particular."
- "I remember what was said, but not what it felt like."

Their accounts are often rich in detail but thin in emotion. You might hear a well-constructed narrative of what happened but feel a surprising lack of affect.

2. Emotional questions fall flat

When asked, "How did that feel at the time?" a client with SDAM might pause and say, "I'm not sure," or "I don't remember."

Even significant or traumatic memories may not come with an emotional imprint. This can be jarring for therapists expecting congruence between story and feeling.

3. They struggle to 'connect the dots' emotionally

Many therapists help clients make links between past and present by emotionally tracing patterns: "This reminds you of how you felt as a child," or "That sounds like the way your father made you feel."

A client with SDAM may struggle to validate that connection. They might say, "I can see the similarity logically, but I don't *feel* it," or "That makes sense, but I don't have an emotional response to it."

This can feel like disconnection, but it's simply the client's memory style.

4. They begin to doubt themselves

Repeated exposure to techniques that require emotional memory may lead to growing client self-doubt. You might hear:

- "Maybe I'm doing this wrong."

- “I feel like I’m not good at therapy.”
- “I must be really repressed.”

If these themes emerge despite the client being otherwise engaged and motivated, it’s worth gently exploring how they experience memory.

5. Visualisation and imagery don’t land

Many clients with SDAM also have aphantasia or low imagery vividness. Even if they don’t, the lack of emotionally charged imagery often makes guided visualisation feel dull or pointless. They may not say it directly, but they may look puzzled, distracted, or apologetic during these exercises.

Therapists might hear:

- “It’s just grey.”
- “I can’t really picture it.”
- “I don’t get anything when I try.”

6. Strong feeling, missing story

Some clients show the reverse pattern: a vivid, specific emotion from the past arrives without the scene it belongs to. They may offer only a factual retelling, or very little at all, of who was there, what was said and how events unfolded, while the feeling itself stays sharp. If that strong feeling is treated as proof that the full memory can be reached, therapist and client can end up searching together for something that isn’t there.

Common misinterpretations: what SDAM isn’t

SDAM is rarely recognised or taught in therapeutic training, so it is frequently misinterpreted through the lens of more familiar frameworks. These misunderstandings can lead to inaccurate formulations, ineffective interventions, and even harm to the therapeutic relationship.

Let's clarify some of the most common misconceptions.

Misread as emotional avoidance

When a client talks about a traumatic experience without strong affect, it is easy to assume they are avoiding or repressing their feelings. Clients with SDAM are not avoiding emotion; many simply can't access the original emotional state associated with the event.

They may know, cognitively, that it was painful. They may understand that others would find it distressing. For many, though, it can't be re-felt, and the absence of emotion is a feature of their autobiographical memory rather than a defence.

Misread as dissociation

Dissociation often presents as a numbing or splitting away from emotion, memory, or self-awareness. Clients with SDAM may sound similarly detached, but their experience is consistent and stable, not episodic or triggered. There is no protective switching off here. The client is reporting their baseline experience of memory.

Unlike dissociation, SDAM doesn't fluctuate with stress or trauma cues. It is a lifelong, trait-level cognitive difference rather than a state-level psychological response.

Misread as a lack of insight

Therapists may assume that a client who can't describe the emotional impact of a memory is lacking in insight or depth. In truth, many clients with SDAM are highly reflective and thoughtful. They may be deeply aware of the consequences of past events and capable of complex meaning-making.

What many of them lack isn't insight but access to emotional re-experiencing. They may understand the "what" and the "why," but the "how it felt" remains elusive.

Misread as a poor therapeutic match

Some therapists begin to question the fit when a client seems disconnected from emotional material. They may wonder if their modality is right, or if the client isn't "ready" for therapy. While it's always appropriate to consider the therapeutic relationship, SDAM doesn't require a different therapist, it requires a different approach.

With the right adaptations, clients with SDAM can engage in rich, effective therapy that honours their cognitive style.

Misread as a trauma block

Perhaps the most damaging misinterpretation is that clients with SDAM are unconsciously blocking traumatic memories. This can lead to unnecessary digging, pathologising, or pressure to access what simply isn't there.

Not everyone who can't remember or re-feel their past is hiding something. For many clients with SDAM, there is no deeper layer of affective content to uncover.

My own history makes this distinction concrete. As a child, my knees dislocated on an all too frequent basis. Even a violent sneeze could do it, and walking on a slippery surface was frightening, because a single slip could take one or both knees out at once.

Double dislocations were a regular part of my childhood. I have no mental memory of the pain. My SDAM means I can only give you the facts of those events, and I can recount them without feeling anything at all, no emotional echo, no physical wince. My body, though, remembers what my mind can't replay. Even now, if my foot slides on a wet floor, the jolt can set off a panic attack and physical intrusions that belong to those childhood dislocations. I understand, logically, exactly what's happening and why. Understanding it doesn't switch it off.

This is what trauma can look like in a client with SDAM. The story arrives flat and factual, and it would be easy to conclude that there is no trauma, or that it's buried beyond reach. Neither is true. Nothing is being blocked; there's simply no episodic recording to retrieve. The trauma lives on in the body and the subconscious, announcing itself in the present through triggers, sensations and alarm responses that carry no retrievable scene. For therapists, this changes the task. The absence of emotional recall doesn't mean the work is finished, and a calm retelling isn't evidence of avoidance. The distress that matters is the distress arriving now, in the body, and it can be worked with directly, without a recovered memory ever needing to surface.

Reframing the work: how to practise when re-living isn't available

If your client can't recall emotionally rich memories, you might wonder, what now? Does that limit the therapeutic journey? Will insight or healing be blocked?

The short answer is no, though it does mean shifting the way we conceptualise and structure our work.

Therapy with clients who have SDAM still reaches depth; the work simply accesses it through different channels.

Start with what is present

Rather than focusing on the emotional content of past experiences, shift attention to:

- Patterns of behaviour over time
- Beliefs formed through lived experience
- Present-day emotional responses
- Values, goals, and meaning making

These are all accessible, even when memory isn't emotionally vivid. In fact, clients with SDAM are often highly attuned to logic, narrative structure, and behavioural insight.

Ask the right questions

Move away from:

- "What did that feel like?"
- "Can you go back to that moment?"
- "What images come to mind?"

Instead, try:

- "What sense have you made of that event since?"
- "What story have you carried about yourself because of that?"
- "What did that experience teach you?"
- "How has that shaped your decisions or relationships?"

These questions keep the work grounded, accessible, and non-shaming. They also build emotional literacy from the outside in.

Use language thoughtfully

You might be surprised how often therapeutic language leans on metaphorical memory:

- "Let's revisit that experience…"
- "Step back into that moment…"
- "Can you visualise how it felt?"

For clients with SDAM, these phrases can cause confusion or internal distress. They may feel they're "doing it wrong" when they don't experience the expected recall.

Instead, try language that invites reflection without presumption:

- "Let's look at that event together."
- "What stands out to you about that time?"
- "When you think about that period in your life, what thoughts come up?"

This gentle shift can help clients feel validated, not excluded.

Work in the present

If the past feels distant or emotionally blank, the present is always alive.

Support clients to:

- Explore current relational dynamics
- Track emotional and physiological responses in real-time
- Notice what triggers particular patterns or reactions
- Develop skills for self-regulation, communication, and decision-making
- Create new stories to override negative ones.

This is especially valuable for clients with SDAM, who may find it easier to reflect on what's happening now than to excavate what happened then.

Support meaning-making, not memory retrieval

Memory isn't the only route to self-awareness. Clients with SDAM can build powerful insight through values clarification, philosophical inquiry, existential exploration, and creative meaning-making.

Ask:

- "What does that say about what matters to you?"
- "How do you want to respond to this pattern now?"
- "What feels most important to take forward from that experience?"

When clients don't know they have SDAM

One of the most significant challenges in working with clients who have SDAM is that many of them don't know they have it.

Unlike more widely recognised cognitive or neurodevelopmental differences, SDAM remains largely unspoken. There's no diagnostic process, no national awareness campaign, no standard screening in therapy intake forms. Most clients with SDAM assume their way of remembering is typical, or worse, believe they are defective because they can't do what others seem to do with ease.

Clients might not say, "I think I have SDAM."

What they *might* say is:

- "I've always had a terrible memory."
- "I remember what happened, but I can't really feel it."

- "My friends talk about re-living moments; I've never experienced that."
- "I can't bring back the emotion, even when I want to."
- "It's like I remember facts, not experiences."

How to open the conversation

It only takes a minute to ask a few illuminating questions:

- "When you think about past experiences, what comes up? Do you see images, feel the emotion, or is it more like facts and knowledge?"
- "Do you tend to re-experience memories, or do you know about them without much emotional or visual detail?"
- "Some people have a memory style that's more factual than sensory, does that sound like you?"

"When a strong feeling shows up, can you usually find the memory it belongs to?"

These questions carry no diagnostic weight. They are invitational, and they say, "It's okay if your mind works differently." For many clients, that's the first time anyone has ever said that to them.

For those who discover SDAM during therapy, the experience can be transformative but also disorienting.

There may be:

- Relief: "There's a name for this! I'm not broken."
- Grief: "I've missed out on something others take for granted."
- Reflection: "No wonder so many things never worked in therapy."
- Hope: "Maybe I can do this differently now."

Supporting a client through this discovery involves validating their experience, gently normalising the cognitive difference, and adjusting your work accordingly.

It's not about labelling but about liberating the client from confusion, or the burden of trying to meet expectations that were never designed for their mind.

Reflective practice

1. *Have you ever had a client who recalled traumatic or significant events with little or no emotional engagement? How did you interpret that?*
2. *In what ways do your preferred methods rely on emotional memory? What might you use instead if those were unavailable?*
3. *How would your approach shift if you knew a client had SDAM? What questions would you ask differently? What outcomes would you expect to change?*
4. *Do you believe that emotional processing can happen without emotional re-living? Why or why not?*

Reflect on the language you use around memory.

Could it be expanded to include clients whose memories are more factual than felt?

Chapter 5

Anauralia and anendophasia: silent minds

The myth of the inner voice

While aphantasia affects our ability to see in our minds, there are other invisible differences that affect how we hear our thoughts and these are anauralia and anendophasia.

When we think about therapeutic frameworks, coaching models, popular psychology, and even everyday language, there is an assumption that everybody has an inner monologue and can hear their thoughts. We speak of our *inner critic*, *self-talk*, or *internal dialogue* as though these are universal experiences. Guided meditations ask us to “listen to what your inner voice is saying,” and therapeutic approaches invite us to “talk to the part of you that's afraid” or “re-write the story in your head.”

What if there's no voice?

What if the mind doesn't narrate, doesn't speak, and doesn't sound like anything at all?

For many people, including myself, that is the reality.

In therapy, this difference often goes unnoticed, until it becomes a barrier. Techniques that rely on imagined dialogue or internal sound fall flat. Clients who think in silence can be misread as evasive, disengaged, or lacking insight, when in fact they are doing their best to work within a system that doesn't fit their cognitive style.

Anauralia and anendophasia are still emerging terms, unfamiliar to many therapists, but profoundly important to the clients who live with them. Without awareness, we risk interpreting silence through the lens of dysfunction. With awareness, we begin to see something else entirely.

To be clear, this reaches well beyond sound. It shapes how we conceptualise thought, how we build relationships with our clients, and how we adapt our methods when the mind we're working with doesn't speak the way we expect.

What are anauralia and anendophasia?

Anauralia and anendophasia are two distinct but closely related cognitive differences that challenge the dominant assumptions about how humans think.

Anauralia refers to the absence of auditory imagery. The term was proposed by Rakshita Hinwar and Anthony Lambert at the University of Auckland in 2021. Individuals with anauralia are unable to mentally replay sound. They can't imagine music playing in their head, hear the voice of a loved one, or summon internal echoes of past conversations. When someone says, "I can still hear their voice," a person with anauralia might smile politely, but the experience is entirely foreign to them. There is no auditory playback, only silence.

Anendophasia, on the other hand, refers specifically to the absence of internal speech. The term was coined by Johanne Nedergaard and Gary Lupyan in 2024. For individuals with this trait, thoughts don't take the form of spoken words in the mind. There is no internal narration. Thoughts still occur, they are present, clear, often highly structured, but they don't pass through language before being expressed.

While these terms are still emerging in both popular and academic discourse, they are becoming increasingly recognised through self-report studies, linguistic pattern research, and anecdotal clusters within the aphantasia community.

It's important to note that anauralia and anendophasia are not the same thing. Some individuals may experience one without the other. For example:

- A person might be able to hear music in their head (no anauralia) but not have an internal monologue (yes to anendophasia).
- Another might have neither: no mental sound and no internal speech.
- A third might have only anauralia but retain internal dialogue.
- A fourth might experience it the same way I do and have anauralia but only partial anendophasia.

There is no hierarchy between these traits, and neither indicates impairment or deficiency in intelligence, memory, or reasoning. They are variations in cognitive experience, variations that profoundly shape how individuals engage with therapy.

Why these definitions matter in therapy

When clients report that they "don't hear their thoughts," therapists often interpret this metaphorically or attribute it to avoidance or detachment. The assumption is that everyone has inner dialogue, and silence is unusual.

In therapy, where many interventions rely on exploring the inner voice, tracking thoughts, challenging internal narratives, engaging in parts work, this distinction becomes crucial. If a client doesn't have internal speech or auditory imagery, then interventions assuming their presence will likely feel alienating, confusing, or ineffective.

Recognising and naming these experiences gives therapists a starting point for adapting their work. It also gives clients something they may never have had before: validation that their silent mind isn't broken, just different.

My silent mind

I often struggle to explain how I think. I can be in a meeting and suddenly know that I have an idea to share but the words only form as they come out of my mouth. My brain subconsciously, silently, formlessly, working on a problem and then presenting a solution to me as I speak. I'm not even sure I can explain to you how I know that there even is an idea. Somehow my conscious gets a nudge that a thought is there ready to be delivered to the world.

For some people this silent thinking is all they have, no inner monologue, no inner dialogue and no inner sound.

Monologue refers to the subconscious voice, that stream of consciousness that you have no control over. That's the one where your inner critic lives.

Dialogue refers to your conscious voice, the one you use to reason and weigh up decisions with. That's the one you have a conversation with on purpose with.

Inner sound is just that, it's the internal sensory representation of sound, like hearing dog barking in your mind.

I do have inner dialogue, which meant that during my breakdown I was able to have conversations with myself about what was happening. I was able to use reason and logic to understand the cause and how to fix that. What I couldn't hear were the subconscious thoughts that were dictating how I was responding emotionally to the situation. Those silent spiralling thoughts that were causing me so much anxiety and stress.

Prevalence and the spectrum of experience

As with aphantasia and SDAM, both anauralia and anendophasia exist along a spectrum. They are not binary states. While some individuals experience a complete absence of auditory imagery or inner speech, others may report limited or inconsistent access to these faculties.

The spectrum: from hyperverbal to silent

- Hyperverbal thinkers often describe an unrelenting inner voice. Their thoughts are narrated, sometimes to the point of exhaustion. These individuals may have multiple overlapping streams of inner speech, an inner monologue, a critical voice, a planning voice, and more.

- Typical verbal thinkers have a steady internal monologue. They hear their thoughts in full sentences and use internal dialogue to problem-solve, reflect, and rehearse conversations.
- Mild anendophasia may manifest as partial inner speech. Some people report only hearing words in emotionally charged situations or when under stress. Others might “hear” single words or vague phrases but not complete sentences. Some may have monologue but no dialogue and vice versa.
- Complete anendophasia means there is no inner speech at all. Thoughts arise fully formed but are not experienced as verbal thoughts.
- Anauralia also varies. Some individuals report hearing certain types of sounds, like music, but not voices. Others might hear the intonation of a sentence but not the words themselves. A complete absence means no sound can be imagined at all. No music, no voices, no remembered auditory detail.

What do we know about prevalence?

Research into these phenomena is still in early stages and because the terms are relatively new and not widely included in clinical assessments, precise statistics are difficult to obtain. However, early surveys conducted by the Aphantasia Network and cognitive psychology labs suggest the following:

- An estimated 5 to 10% of people may experience partial or complete anendophasia.

- Roughly 10 to 15% of people may report low auditory imagery, with a smaller subset experiencing full anauralia.
- Co-occurrence with aphantasia is common. Many individuals who can't visualise also report little or no internal sound or speech.

If we conservatively estimate that 5% of the global population experiences one or both of these traits, that will still equate to roughly 410 million people worldwide at the time of writing. That isn't rare and is statistically significant.

Yet, these differences remain almost entirely unacknowledged in therapy training and clinical practice. They are hiding in plain sight.

How does this present in therapy?

The spectrum of internal experience can result in varying degrees of difficulty with common therapeutic tools. For example:

- A client with mild anendophasia might struggle with journaling but can still identify key thoughts after some reflection.
- A client with complete anauralia may find guided meditation or auditory imagery distressing or meaningless.
- A client with both may present as disconnected, not because they lack self-awareness, but because the questions posed don't align with how their mind processes experience. They may seem slow to answer as they try to uncover thoughts and that could be taken as avoidance or resistance.

Recognising where a client sits on this spectrum allows therapists to tailor their interventions with greater accuracy and empathy.

Neuroscience and what the brain tells us

Scientific understanding of anauralia and anendophasia is still developing, but emerging evidence suggests these differences are both real and measurable, rooted not in psychology or trauma, but in cognitive and neurological variation.

The inner voice and the brain

In neurotypical individuals, inner speech activates several key brain regions:

- The left inferior frontal gyrus, also known as Broca's area, which is responsible for speech production.
- The supplementary motor area, associated with the planning of movement, including the imagined movement of speaking.
- The auditory cortex, particularly the left superior temporal gyrus, which becomes active even when a person is just imagining hearing speech.

In studies using functional MRI (fMRI) and magnetoencephalography (MEG), these areas show activation when participants are asked to silently read or imagine their own voice. This suggests that even imagined speech follows a recognisable neural pathway.

In individuals with anendophasia, this activation pattern is significantly diminished or absent. When asked to engage in tasks that typically provoke inner speech, their brains don't light up in the same areas, or not to the same degree.

This isn't indicative of a disorder; it simply reflects a different cognitive pathway.

Brain differences, not brain damage

It's important to note that these are not signs of impairment. In fact, people with silent minds often excel in other areas, including abstract reasoning, spatial logic, and problem-solving.

Some studies suggest that individuals without inner speech may rely more heavily on the default mode network, a set of brain regions associated with daydreaming, non-linear thinking, and conceptual processing. Rather than thinking in words, they may think in symbols, connections, or intuitive insights.

This helps explain why so many clients with anendophasia or anauralia are highly intelligent, articulate, and capable, yet feel alienated by therapy models that assume they can "talk to themselves" in the way others can.

Neuroscience validates this experience

The emerging consensus is that internal dialogue isn't universal. It isn't a prerequisite for thought, and where it is absent, we are not looking at a deficit, but at a different mode of cognition.

For therapists, this research offers something powerful: validation. You don't need to rely on gut instinct alone when a client says they can't access an inner voice. The neuroscience backs them up.

When clients can't talk to themselves: therapeutic consequences

Much of modern therapy is built on the assumption that clients can observe and articulate their inner world through some form of internal dialogue. We invite clients to "tune in," "listen to the voice of anxiety," or "challenge their inner critic." What happens when those voices are not there to be heard?

Techniques that depend on inner speech

The following approaches are just a few examples of how therapy assumes an internal linguistic process:

- Cognitive Behavioural Therapy (CBT) often involves identifying and disputing negative automatic thoughts. This requires the client to be able to detect an internal monologue.
- Internal Family Systems (IFS) assumes that the self is composed of internal parts in dialogue with one another.
- Narrative Therapy invites clients to externalise and revise their internal stories, with the presumption that a story already exists in language form.
- Compassion-Focused Therapy (CFT) often encourages clients to generate soothing self-talk or compassionate internal phrases.
- Psychodynamic approaches may work with transference through imagined conversations with parental figures or past selves.
- Mindfulness and ACT often invite noticing of "mental chatter" or "storytelling."

Each of these relies on at least some capacity for inner speech or imagined sound.

The impact on the therapeutic process

When a client doesn't have an internal voice, the result is often an uncomfortable therapeutic mismatch. It may look like:

- Blankness during parts work: The client has no way to 'hear' or 'speak to' parts of themselves.
- Confusion in CBT: They can't "catch" negative thoughts because they don't experience them as verbal or structured.
- Frustration during journaling: Writing feels like trying to translate something that never had words.
- Alienation in CFT: Soothing phrases don't emerge naturally, and imagined compassion feels hollow or forced.
- Shame or self-doubt: The client begins to feel that they must be doing therapy wrong.

They may say things like:

- "I'm not sure what that part would say."
- "I don't have an inner critic, I just feel bad."
- "I didn't really think anything, I just reacted."
- "I know I should write things down, but I never know what to say."

None of these signals avoidance or unwillingness. Each points to a mind that doesn't process experience through inner language.

The risk of misinterpretation

Without awareness of silent mind profiles, therapists may mislabel a lack of inner speech as:

- Resistance
- Avoidance

- Emotional shutdown
- Lack of psychological insight
- Poor emotional intelligence
- Disconnection from self

None of these interpretations are accurate or helpful and they can deeply harm the therapeutic alliance.

When clients sense that they are being pathologised for something they can't do, and have never done, they often begin to mask. They might fabricate internal dialogue, invent parts, or echo language the therapist has introduced, simply to stay connected. The cost is high: emotional authenticity is sacrificed, and therapeutic depth becomes unreachable.

Silence isn't emptiness

Clients with silent minds are not empty. They may be reflecting deeply, experiencing fully, and processing in profound ways, just not through words.

Their self-awareness may be bodily, emotional, relational, or abstract. They may know what they believe, understand patterns, and hold meaningful insights, but none of this is packaged in internal language. Instead, it may come through:

- Gestures or posture
- Changes in tone or energy
- Imagery or metaphor
- A strong sense of what feels right or wrong
- An intuitive understanding of systems, people, or dynamics
- A simple 'knowing'

The shape of silent cognition

For clients with anendophasia and anauralia, the absence of inner voice or sound doesn't mean an absence of thought. It simply means their thoughts don't arrive in words, tones, or mental rehearsals. Instead, cognition emerges in different shapes, often less linear, but no less profound.

Some describe their thinking as a kind of internal blueprint. They hold a web of concepts, relationships, and logical structures in their mind, but without narrating them. Others speak of "knowing all at once" rather than reasoning step-by-step. It's less like telling yourself a story and more like seeing the pattern.

This kind of cognition is:

- Spatial: Information is held and moved through as if on a mental map.
- Conceptual: Abstract ideas come fully formed, rather than through verbal processing.
- Emotional or embodied: Thoughts are accompanied by a sense of 'rightness', a shift in physical sensation, or an emotional cue, not a sentence.

These clients often don't process experiences by "talking them through" internally before speaking aloud. Instead, what they say is often being constructed in real time. There was no script. There was no rehearsal. This can result in moments of hesitation or frustration, not because they're holding back, but because the translation from knowing to speaking takes effort.

Understanding this helps therapists avoid mislabelling clients as slow to open up or uncertain. Silent cognition is just that, silent.

Beneath the quiet, though, there is often a rich internal framework of insight, pattern recognition, and deep feeling that can be accessed through different routes.

Daniel's story

Daniel, a 35-year-old data analyst, sought therapy for recurring burnout and low self-worth. Highly analytical and reserved, he had spent years excelling professionally while feeling increasingly isolated and emotionally numb. His presenting concerns included overthinking, decision fatigue, and a persistent sense of not knowing what he wanted from life.

His therapist, trained in CBT and parts-based work, began by exploring Daniel's internal dialogue. In early sessions, they focused on identifying the 'inner critic' and tracking negative self-talk, but Daniel consistently struggled to engage.

"What does that negative voice in your mind say to you when you make a mistake? What are you subconsciously saying to yourself?"

Daniel paused. "I don't know. I don't think it says anything."

"Okay, what does it feel like?"

"It just feels… bad. I know I've done something wrong. I don't really know what I'm thinking when it happens"

His therapist gently encouraged him to imagine what that part might sound like, what it might say. Daniel tried, he really did, but the exercise felt like theatre. There was no voice, just a sinking feeling and a desire to withdraw.

As the sessions progressed, Daniel began to feel increasingly frustrated. He couldn't do what he was being asked to do. "Maybe I'm just too closed off," he said once. "Maybe I don't know myself well enough."

Midway through the therapy process, Daniel stumbled across an article on aphantasia. Curious, he kept reading and discovered something called anendophasia, a term he had never encountered before. The description resonated. He didn't talk to himself in his head. He never had. His thoughts came fully formed, often as conclusions or gut decisions, but never in verbal sentences. Armed with this insight, Daniel brought the article to therapy. His therapist, open and willing to learn, took it seriously. They began to reframe the work, not as an attempt to elicit inner speech, but to explore what Daniel did experience.

Instead of asking what his inner critic said, the therapist asked:

"What happens in your body when you notice that sinking feeling?"

"If you had to draw or shape that feeling, what would it look like?"

"How do you usually know when something's wrong?"

With these shifts, Daniel started to engage more meaningfully. He mapped his internal states through imagery, movement, and metaphor. He used logic and value-based reflection instead of imagined self-talk. The room felt safer. The silence, no longer suspicious, became a place of insight.

By the end of therapy, Daniel wasn't "fixed", but he no longer felt broken. He understood himself better. He had tools that fit. Most importantly, he felt genuinely seen.

Gentle inquiry without assumption

One of the most important shifts a therapist can make when working with clients who may have anauralia or anendophasia is to drop the assumption that inner speech or sound is a given. Inquiry becomes a process of discovery, not confirmation. Instead of asking questions that presume a particular type of cognition, we invite the client to show us how their mind works on their terms.

Here are some examples of curiosity-led, inclusive questions:

- "When you think something through, what does that feel like internally?"
- "Do your thoughts show up as words, pictures, emotions, or something else entirely?"
- "Some people have a voice in their head, like an inner narrator. Others don't. What's it like for you?"
- "When you remember something, do you hear it, see it, or just know it happened?"
- "How do you usually make decisions? Is it more of a gut feeling, a sense of knowing, or something else?"

These questions do two things. First, they open a door to self-awareness for the client, many of whom may never have considered how they think before. Second, they communicate to the client that there is no wrong answer and that their mind is welcome here, even if it doesn't speak the way others do.

This kind of inquiry also builds trust. When a therapist asks about cognition without judgement, it signals that the work ahead will be collaborative rather than corrective. It tells the client: "You don't need to pretend. You don't need to perform. I want to understand you as you are."

It also protects the therapeutic alliance. Clients with silent minds often fear that their difference will be pathologised. They may have spent years trying to fit themselves into cognitive frameworks that never quite fit. Gentle, open-ended inquiry gives them permission to be honest, and often, for the first time, to be understood.

Adaptations that help

When therapists learn that a client doesn't think in words or imagine sounds, it can feel disorientating at first, particularly if much of their training has emphasised techniques based on internal dialogue. This moment of uncertainty is also a moment of possibility, because once we release the need for inner speech, a broader range of therapeutic tools becomes available.

Here are several practical ways to adapt your approach for clients with anauralia or anendophasia:

1. Use visual and tactile metaphors

Rather than asking clients to name or dialogue with a part of themselves, invite them to give it shape or presence. For example:

- "If that anxious feeling had a shape or texture, what would it be?"
- "Could we represent that stuckness using an object or image?"

This allows emotional content to be explored symbolically rather than linguistically.

2. Work with felt sense and body awareness

Clients who can't articulate an inner voice often have a strong connection to bodily cues. You might ask:

- "Where do you feel that in your body?"
- "If that sensation had a movement or a sound outside of you, what might it be?"

This taps into non-verbal processing without requiring imagined speech.

3. Encourage external expression

For silent mind clients, inner dialogue may not be accessible, but external dialogue can still be productive. Try:

- Drawing or sketching feelings or patterns.
- Using physical objects (e.g. stones, tokens, cards) to represent internal states or relational dynamics.
- Inviting short, spoken reflections to clarify emerging insights, rather than asking for introspective narrative.

4. Frame insight as emergent, not rehearsed

Many silent-minded clients describe their spoken words as arriving in real-time. They may not "know" what they think until they say it aloud. Create space for this by:

- Slowing the pace.
- Normalising pauses and silence.
- Using prompts like, "Let's see what comes up when you try to put it into words."

5. Value pattern recognition over verbal reflection

Rather than focusing on what a part might "say," explore:

- Recurring behaviours or automatic responses.
- Triggers and reactions.

- Shifts in energy or engagement.

This can lead to rich therapeutic work without requiring inner narrative.

6. Support clients to develop their own language

Clients with anendophasia may struggle with typical journaling but still benefit from expressive practices. Help them experiment with:

- Sentence stems or prompt-based reflection.
- Voice notes if speaking is easier than writing.
- Diagrams, flowcharts, or timelines to externalise process.

The goal isn't fluency in inner speech, but fluency in *expression*, whatever form that takes.

7. Name and normalise this experience

Often, the most powerful intervention is simply to name the difference and reassure the client that it's not a problem. Phrases like:

- "You're not doing it wrong. Your mind just works differently."
- "There's no one right way to reflect."
- "Let's find tools that suit your way of thinking."

These small reframes can release shame and create spaciousness in the work.

Reflective practice

1. *Have you ever worked with a client who struggled to identify or describe an inner voice? What assumptions did you make in response?*
2. *Think about your own internal experience. Do you hear your thoughts in words? How might that influence the way you interpret silence?*
3. *How do your current techniques rely on internal dialogue or imagined sound? What would it look like to offer alternative routes to insight?*
4. *If a client says, "I don't have an inner voice," how might you respond without trying to fix, translate, or override their experience?*
5. *Reflect on the language you use in sessions. Could phrases like "tune in," "listen to your gut," or "what is that part saying?" unintentionally exclude clients who think in different ways?*
6. *What new questions could you ask that welcome cognitive diversity into the room?*

Write down one practical change you could make to ensure clients with silent minds feel recognised in your practice.

Chapter 6

Alexithymia: unfelt emotions

"I don't know how I feel"

It's a phrase therapists hear often. Sometimes it's fleeting, a moment of emotional overwhelm, a sign that a client isn't yet ready to go deeper. Other times, it's interpreted as a kind of psychological resistance: a client who is shut down, defended, or emotionally disconnected. What if it's neither? What if it's simply the truth?

What if the client genuinely can't identify, name, or describe their emotional state. Not because they are avoiding it, but because their brain doesn't give them access to it in the way we expect.

For many people, "I don't know how I feel" isn't a temporary state. It's a constant feature of their inner world, and in therapy, it can become a point of confusion, frustration, or even rupture, especially when therapists try to interpret it using the wrong map.

This chapter is about one of the most misunderstood differences in therapeutic work: alexithymia.

Alexithymia describes people who have trouble recognising, understanding, and putting their emotions into words.

Alexithymia reflects a difference in how the brain processes emotion, specifically in how it integrates emotional signals into conscious awareness and language. It can be present as a standalone trait or occur alongside other neurodivergent profiles, such as autism, ADHD, SDAM, aphantasia, or interoceptive differences. It is also more common than many therapists realise.

Therapy is built on the assumption that people *can* access their emotional world, and that growth comes through naming, exploring, and working with those feelings. For clients with alexithymia, that assumption can create tension. When the therapist pushes for clarity, the client doesn't possess, the result can be withdrawal, shame, or masking.

I remember vividly one of my own early therapy sessions, when my therapist gently asked, "How do you feel right now?" I paused. I scanned. I searched. I knew I was having a reaction, my body was tense, my chest tight, but I didn't know how to answer. There were no words, no clean labels, just a cloud of unease. When I said, "I don't know," they smiled kindly and said, "Take your time, it's safe to go there." I wasn't afraid to go there, though. There was simply nowhere to go.

I didn't have words, beyond the physical sensations, to explain what I was feeling.

This chapter is for therapists who've felt puzzled when a client couldn't engage with emotional work the way they expected. It's for those who've questioned a client's readiness, or their own skill. It's also for the many clients who've left sessions wondering what's wrong with them when the answer may be nothing at all.

Some clients don't process emotion in the way therapy expects and when we learn to recognise that difference, a whole new path to connection, insight, and therapeutic growth opens up.

Core features of alexithymia

1. Difficulty identifying emotions.

People with alexithymia often experience emotional arousal, tightness in the chest, a racing heart, tears, or fatigue, but can't confidently name what they're feeling. They may struggle to distinguish between anger and anxiety, or between grief and overwhelm. The sensation is there, but the label is missing.

2. Difficulty describing emotions.

Even when there is a sense of feeling *something*, the ability to put that feeling into words may be limited or absent. Clients may use vague or generic language ("weird," "off," "not right") or avoid emotional terms altogether. Attempts to journal or share their inner world may result in frustration or intellectual detours.

3. Difficulty distinguishing between physical and emotional states.

For some, emotional responses are somatised, felt more in the body than in the mind. A knot in the stomach might signal fear, guilt, or simply hunger. Fatigue might stem from sadness, depression, or physical illness. Without a clear emotional reference point, these internal signals remain ambiguous and difficult to interpret.

Not a disorder, but a difference, it is essential to recognise that alexithymia isn't classified as a mental illness. It may occur in individuals with no other diagnostic labels or alongside:

- Autism
- ADHD
- PTSD or complex trauma histories
- Depression and anxiety
- Eating disorders
- Substance use disorders

However, its presence isn't necessarily indicative of dysfunction. Many people with alexithymia live rich, meaningful lives and possess high levels of intelligence, empathy, and reflective ability, just not through the emotional channels that traditional therapy often prioritises.

Why this definition matters in therapy

Without a clear understanding of alexithymia as a *neurological variation* rather than a *psychological avoidance*, therapists risk pathologising silence, mistaking difficulty with emotional language as resistance, or framing bodily-based responses as shutdown. These misinterpretations can lead to therapeutic rupture, missed opportunities, or a quiet sense of failure for both therapist and client.

When we name alexithymia accurately, we create space for difference. We shift the question from *"Why won't this client talk about their feelings?"* to *"What would emotional exploration look like in a mind that processes emotion differently?",* and that's the beginning of more inclusive, attuned, and effective work.

The hidden prevalence

More people experience alexithymia than many therapists realise. It is not rare, obscure or confined to clinical populations; it is a trait affecting a large portion of the public and, by extension, a significant portion of therapy clients.

Current research suggests that around 10% of the general population meet criteria for clinically significant alexithymia. That equates to millions of individuals worldwide who live with limited access to their emotional vocabulary.

These individuals may never present for mental health support. Or they may seek it for difficulties that mask the underlying issue, relationship problems, burnout, anxiety, or psychosomatic symptoms that are compounded by their lack of emotional clarity.

Higher prevalence in neurodivergent and trauma-affected populations

While 10% is a meaningful baseline, rates of alexithymia rise significantly in specific populations:

- Autism: Studies suggest that up to 50% of autistic individuals exhibit moderate to high levels of alexithymia. This overlap is so strong that it is often mistaken for a core feature of autism itself, yet many researchers now argue that alexithymia should be considered a separate but co-occurring trait.
- PTSD and complex trauma: People with histories of trauma often experience alexithymia-like symptoms. In some cases, this may be a result of emotional shutdown or survival-based disconnection. In others, it may reflect an underlying trait that predates the trauma, making emotional processing more difficult to begin with.
- Aphantasia and SDAM: There is a growing body of anecdotal and emerging research evidence linking alexithymia to other forms of cognitive difference. Individuals with aphantasia and SDAM frequently report alexithymic traits, likely because all three affect internal access to lived experience, whether visual, emotional, or narrative. While exact statistics are still

being refined, co-occurrence in these populations appears to be well above average.

A common experience in the therapy room

For therapists, this means one thing above all: you are almost certainly already working with clients with alexithymia, whether you know it or not.

They may not use the term. They may not describe themselves in those words. They might consistently say:

- “I don’t know how I feel.”
- “It’s hard to explain.”
- “I just feel weird.”
- “It’s more physical than emotional.”

These clients often fly under the radar. They show up, engage to the best of their ability, and mask their confusion or disconnection by trying to “get therapy right.” They may intellectualise, avoid emotional prompts, or silently carry the shame of not accessing feelings the way others seem to do so effortlessly.

Far from a fringe experience, alexithymia hides in plain sight, and the more we recognise its prevalence, the better we can adapt our methods, language, and expectations to serve the clients already in our care.

What alexithymia feels like (from the inside)

Imagine trying to name colours in a fog. You see the fog and you know that colours are there, but you can’t quite see them clearly enough to name them. You squint, you guess, you reach for language, but nothing fits. You know you're seeing *something*, but you don't know what.

This is often what alexithymia feels like from the inside.

For many people with alexithymia, emotions exist, but they arrive unlabelled. They are sensed but not known, experienced but not easily named. A growing tightness in the chest might be fear, or anger, or sadness, or just a sign that something's wrong. Without the language to capture it, the experience floats just outside of conscious grasp.

For some the challenge is to even identify that there is a feeling. Chest tightness goes unrecognised, the physical sensations are flat, unfelt.

It's like receiving signals with the volume turned down and the subtitles missing. You catch fragments, but the full message never comes through.

Neither numb nor avoidant, simply different

A common misunderstanding is to conflate alexithymia with emotional numbness, but they are not the same.

- Emotional numbness often reflects a *psychological defence*, a shutting down in response to pain or trauma. It usually has a before-and-after. Something happened, and the person stopped feeling.
- Alexithymia, by contrast, is a *trait*. It may have been present since early life or developed over time. Clients may have never been able to name their emotions clearly.

Another key distinction is between not feeling and not recognising.

People with alexithymia do feel. They may become tearful during films, feel overwhelmed in crowds, or lash out in frustration, but they struggle to *track* or *understand* what they're feeling until it reaches a tipping point. There's a disconnect between internal signals and conscious awareness.

They may describe this as:

- "A background noise I can't quite hear."
- "Something building up until it explodes."
- "A fog in my body that I only realise afterwards."

They notice the *impact* of emotion before the emotion itself, withdrawal from social contact, sleep disturbance, tension in the shoulders, irritability. The feelings are real, but their form is elusive.

When language fails, people often stop trying. Many clients with alexithymia report giving up on expressing how they feel because it never seemed to come out right. They worry about sounding vague, dramatic, or inauthentic. Some learn to avoid emotional conversations altogether, not because they are unwilling to go there, but because the journey always feels half-blind.

For these clients, therapy can feel like being asked to describe a song they've only ever heard through a wall.

Yet when therapists slow down, drop the pressure, and allow space for *felt sense*, metaphor, or behaviour-based reflection, something remarkable happens. The fog doesn't necessarily lift but the client realises they're not alone in it and sometimes that is enough to begin.

Emotional expression vs emotional experience

One of the most important distinctions to make when working with alexithymia is between having an emotional experience and being able to express or reflect on it.

They are not the same thing. A client may *feel deeply* yet appear emotionally flat in conversation. They may cry without knowing why, react strongly to relational stress but be unable to explain it, or seem disconnected even while sitting with overwhelming emotional activation.

The disconnect sits between the emotion itself and the ability to track, label, or translate that experience into language. Suppression and resistance play no part in it.

Therapists are often trained to ask questions like:

- "How did that make you feel?"
- "What's coming up emotionally right now?"
- "Can you name what that sensation is?"

These are useful questions for clients who process emotion through language and introspection, but for those with alexithymia, such questions can feel like being asked to describe a shape that hasn't yet emerged. The feeling is there, but it remains unformed, unnamed, and often ungraspable in the moment.

They may say:

- "I don't know."
- "It just felt… off."
- "It's like I've emotionally flatlined, I just don't feel anything."

It's not that they *didn't* have an emotional experience. It's that they can't pull it into consciousness with the clarity therapy often requires.

It's important to remember that emotional expression is a skill, one that is developed through socialisation, cultural modelling, and often neurotypical pathways. Clients with alexithymia may not have learned this skill in a way that fits conventional expectations. They may have been raised in emotionally restricted environments, or their brains may simply not organise experience through affective language.

Similarly, emotional reflection, the ability to look inward, interpret one's state, and derive meaning, is a layered process. It relies on more than just emotion. It requires working memory, cognitive flexibility, and often visual, auditory, or linguistic cues. If those are absent or reduced, reflection becomes difficult, even if the emotional experience itself is profound.

Clients might know:

- "I was upset,"
- "It affected me for days,"
- "I couldn't sleep,"

When asked why, or how, or what exactly was felt, the answers falter.

The risk of missing what's there

When therapists equate emotional insight with emotional depth, clients with alexithymia can be unfairly seen as shallow or emotionally unavailable. This is a mistake.

They may carry strong emotional histories, they may be living with grief, shame, longing, or anger that they can't easily name. They may be experiencing all the physical responses but not be able to notice them, and they may be acutely sensitive to mood, tone, and interpersonal tension, even while unable to describe what it stirs inside them.

When we separate emotional experience from emotional expression, we create space for these clients to be understood, not just evaluated.

In that space, they can begin to build a bridge between what is *felt*, and what might one day be *said*.

Neuroscience of alexithymia

For many clients with alexithymia, the struggle to identify, interpret, and articulate emotion feels frustratingly opaque. They know something is happening internally, but they can't access it with clarity or language. Far from being psychological resistance or emotional immaturity, this pattern appears to have a clear neurological basis.

Functional MRI (fMRI) studies have revealed measurable differences in the brains of people with alexithymia, particularly in the connectivity between three key areas:

- The anterior insula: responsible for processing internal bodily states (interoception).
- The anterior cingulate cortex (ACC): involved in emotional regulation and attention.
- The prefrontal cortex: essential for higher-order thinking and conscious reflection.

In individuals with alexithymia, communication between these areas tends to be reduced. What this means in practice is that signals from the body, such as a racing heart, tight chest, or sinking stomach, may not be efficiently translated into emotional awareness. The sensation is there, but the brain struggles to make sense of it in psychological terms. There is input, but no label.

This links closely to interoception, our ability to notice and interpret internal bodily cues. For someone without alexithymia, a tight chest might automatically register as anxiety, a warm flush as embarrassment, or a tension headache as unresolved frustration. For someone with alexithymia, those signals can feel more like generalised noise: discomfort without context.

Researchers have also explored somatic marker theory, the idea that our bodies provide intuitive, pre-verbal cues that guide decision-making and emotional responses. These somatic markers (gut feelings, heart rate shifts, bodily tension) are thought to play a crucial role in emotional awareness. In alexithymic individuals, however, these markers tend to be muted or misread. The physiological response occurs, but it doesn't connect to conscious emotion in a typical way.

Importantly, these neurological findings reinforce what many clients have long suspected: they are not out of touch because they are unwilling, nor are they emotionally shallow or avoiding depth. Their brains are simply processing internal data differently and when therapy relies on insight that presumes typical interoception or emotional fluency, it creates a mismatch that can undermine the work.

The gift of this emerging science is validation. For clients, it means they're not alone, and they're not broken. For therapists, it means we can start to let go of outdated assumptions and begin to meet clients where they truly are, using approaches that honour their cognitive and emotional reality.

Therapy and the demand for emotional fluency

Much of contemporary therapy rests on a quiet but powerful assumption: that emotional insight is both possible and necessary. We are trained to guide clients towards greater emotional literacy, to encourage naming and tracking feelings, and to interpret emotional patterns as clues to deeper psychological material. Progress is often measured in affective terms, "How did that feel?" "Where do you notice that in your body?" "What happens when you stay with that feeling?"

Many therapeutic approaches implicitly assume a baseline level of emotional fluency:

- Emotion-Focused Therapy (EFT) relies on accessing, expressing, and processing core emotional states.
- Reflective journaling assumes that clients can articulate feelings and gain insight through self-exploration.
- Empathy-building techniques, such as perspective-taking or relational attunement, expect an ability to feel with and for others, something that may be present, but difficult to name or explain.
- Somatic and trauma-based approaches often encourage clients to notice physical sensations and connect them to emotional states, an impossible task when the distinction between the two is unclear or inaccessible.

Even in general integrative work, there is often an unspoken hierarchy: emotional awareness is seen as the gold standard, and cognitive insight alone is viewed as insufficient or superficial. This creates a double bind for the alexithymic client. They may be deeply reflective, behaviourally self-aware, and capable of significant change, but still feel like they are failing the unspoken test of "feeling enough."

Therapists may find themselves struggling too. A client who can't access emotion may seem evasive or detached. A flat effect can feel unsettling. Vague or somatic descriptions might be misread as reluctance, guardedness, or intellectualisation. Over time, this can trigger frustration or self-doubt in the therapist, "Am I doing something wrong?" "Why can't we get deeper?"

To work effectively with alexithymic clients, we must de-centre emotional fluency as the primary metric of therapeutic success. Growth can occur through insight, values clarification, behaviour change, and meaning making, even if the client can't tell you how they feel. Emotional depth may still be present, just not in ways that fit conventional formats.

Therapy isn't just for those who speak the language of emotion fluently. It is also for those learning how to translate silence, sensation, or confusion into something meaningful.

Recognising alexithymia and avoiding misinterpretation

Alexithymia rarely announces itself. It doesn't arrive with a label or diagnosis. More often, it shows up quietly, through mismatched expectations, therapeutic misunderstandings, and moments that don't quite land. For many therapists, the first sign that something is different is a subtle sense of disconnection.

A client appears thoughtful, perhaps even engaged, but when asked how they feel, they pause. They search for words. They say, "I don't know." Their language is flat or vague. Emotional detail is sparse. Or they describe their emotional state in physical terms, "tight chest," "weird feeling," "just off."

Rather than an emotional narrative, they offer logic. Rather than insight into feelings, they offer timelines, decisions, or behavioural observations.

These moments can be misread, especially when therapists aren't yet familiar with alexithymia.

Common presentations of alexithymia

- Flat affect: The client's emotional tone may appear muted or neutral, even when discussing significant life events.
- Vague language: Descriptions of emotion are imprecise or nonspecific, "weird," "meh," "just not right."
- Somatic substitution: Feelings are framed in bodily terms, pressure, tightness, headaches, tension.
- Cognitive preference: The client gravitates towards logical analysis, patterns, or behaviour rather than internal emotional states.
- Short answers in emotional inquiry: "I don't know." "Not sure." "Nothing really."

None of these indicate lack of depth or care, but they can lead to problematic assumptions.

Common therapist misinterpretations

- "They're intellectualising": While some clients do use thought to avoid feeling, alexithymic clients often process through cognition by default, not defence.
- "They're emotionally avoidant": Avoidance implies that something is being hidden or pushed away. In alexithymia, it may not be accessible in the first place.
- "They're not connecting": Connection may still be happening, just not through emotional dialogue.
- "They're resistant": Resistance presumes refusal. Alexithymia is a difference, not a refusal.

When we pathologise the difference, we risk rupturing the relationship. The client may begin to feel judged or pressured. They may mask, guessing at emotional language that doesn't feel true, or they may quietly disengage.

Reframes and red flags for the attuned therapist

- Reframe silence as information: If a client can't name a feeling, explore how they know something is happening at all. What cues do they notice?
- Treat "I don't know" as a starting point, not a wall: Ask what they do know, or how they've learned to tell when something is off.
- Replace "What are you feeling?" with "What's your sense of what's going on?" This opens the door to knowing without requiring emotional fluency.

- Watch for consistency: If the client always gives physical or behavioural descriptions without emotional insight, alexithymia may be at play.
- Believe them: If they say they don't know what they feel, take it at face value. This belief alone can be profoundly regulating.

Recognition allows for adaptation and adaptation is the bridge between difference and attunement.

Rather than a barrier to therapy, alexithymia is a cue to shift our frame. These clients are often highly motivated and deeply engaged but their path to growth may not follow the usual map. It is our role to honour the route they do take.

Laura's story

Laura, a 38-year-old creative business owner, sought therapy for ongoing relationship stress, burnout, and difficulty "switching off." She described herself as highly self-aware, observant, and good at helping others, but admitted that when it came to her own emotions, she often felt confused and disconnected.

In early sessions, Laura was articulate and reflective. She spoke about her experiences in detail, including childhood dynamics, recent conflicts, and the pressures of running a business, but when the conversation turned to emotion, something shifted.

"How did that feel for you?" her therapist asked gently.

Laura frowned, searching for the right words. "I don't know. It was just... a lot"

Over several sessions, this pattern repeated. Laura reported intense physical sensations, headaches, muscle tension, breathlessness, nausea, but consistently struggled to link these to emotional states. When asked to use feeling words, she often guessed. "Maybe sad? Or angry? I don't know. Whatever it was, I didn't like it."

Despite her willingness to engage, Laura began to feel like she was failing therapy. "I know I should be more in touch with my emotions," she said, "but I'm just not." She worried that she was emotionally repressed or too analytical. "One of my closest friends once said I have a heart of stone"

Her therapist, at first, considered this might be a defence, possibly related to past trauma or avoidant attachment but something didn't quite fit. Laura was open. She wasn't dodging or guarded. She simply didn't seem to have access to the emotional language or signals that most clients relied on. She wasn't keeping her feelings out; she couldn't reach them.

This prompted her therapist to explore a different framework. After some research and reflection, the therapist introduced the concept of alexithymia, the possibility that Laura's difficulties weren't about avoidance.

Laura was relieved. For the first time, she had language for an experience she had never been able to articulate. She didn't feel broken, just different and she understood that difference didn't mean bad.

With this shift in understanding, the therapist adapted her approach. Rather than pressing for emotional labels, she asked broader questions:

- *"What does this situation mean to you?"*
- *"If this experience were a colour or shape, what might it be?"*
- *"What happens in your body when this state shows up?"*
- *"Are there patterns in your responses you've started to notice?"*

Instead of trying to name feelings, Laura began identifying patterns. She noticed when certain bodily sensations arose. She linked these to situations, triggers, and decisions. Through metaphor, story, and values-based exploration, she found new ways to understand herself.

By the end of therapy, Laura still didn't have easy access to emotional vocabulary, but she no longer saw that as a flaw. She had developed a more nuanced awareness of her internal world and, most importantly, she had stopped masking. She trusted that her way of processing was valid, and her therapist did too.

Working with (not against) alexithymia

It can be tempting, especially in emotionally focused therapies, to treat alexithymia as something to overcome.

You can't train someone out of alexithymia, but you can help them to explore their emotional world, develop the tools to identify and name their own emotions and the emotions of others. You can't coax emotional fluency where the underlying cognitive mechanisms for emotional identification and labelling are absent or muted, but you can build bridges. You can support clients in creating new frameworks for self-understanding, using the language and methods that *do* make sense to them.

Here are a few key adaptations that can help:

Externalising tools

Clients with alexithymia often benefit from concrete, visual, or embodied prompts that bypass the demand for spontaneous emotional vocabulary.

- Emotion wheels or charts offer a visual menu of feeling words to help with tentative exploration. The goal isn't to force a match, but to invite curiosity.
- Feeling cards or word banks allow clients to point or select rather than generate from within.
- Somatic prompts, such as body maps or movement-based check-ins ("Where do you feel that in your body?"), can provide an alternative route into emotional awareness, but only when framed gently and without assumption.
- Metaphor or sensory-based cues, e.g., "Does this feeling have a temperature?" or "What shape does this remind you of?", can help clients describe their inner state without needing precise emotional labels.

Naming patterns, not feelings

Rather than asking, "How do you feel when that happens?" try, "What tends to happen when that situation arises?"

Clients with alexithymia are often skilled at recognising external patterns:

- “When I feel that pressure in my chest, I usually withdraw.”
- “Every time someone challenges me, I get really tired afterwards.”
- “When I’m overwhelmed, I overwork rather than rest.”

These behavioural and physical patterns are valid and meaningful, even without named emotions attached. They provide insight into needs, triggers, and coping styles that can be therapeutically powerful.

Therapists can support clients in gently expanding their emotional language without pressuring them to become fluent.

This might involve:

- Introducing one or two new feeling words at a time and exploring what they *might* mean together
- Offering stories, poems, or fictional characters and asking, “Does any of this resonate?”
- Reflecting client language back without reframing it too quickly, e.g., “You said it feels weird and heavy. Let’s stay with that. What kind of heavy?”

Over time, the client may begin to form internal links between bodily sensations, experiences, and symbolic language. This will be their process, though, not one imposed from outside.

Values, actions, and meaning

When emotions are hard to access, therapy can find firm ground in values and action.

- “What matters most to you in this situation?”
- “What kind of person do you want to be in this moment?”

- "What does this reaction seem to be protecting or pointing towards?"

These are emotionally significant questions that don't rely on feeling words. They help clients anchor themselves in meaning and purpose, which can, in turn, provide a sense of emotional coherence, even when the feelings remain hard to name.

The key shift for therapists is to stop chasing the emotion. Start listening to the way your client already makes sense of their experience. Emotion isn't the only door to healing. Sometimes, the path in is lined with logic, sensation, metaphor, and meaning and that path is no less valid.

Therapist challenges and opportunities

Working with clients who have alexithymia can evoke a range of responses in therapists, some of which are difficult to name, and others that touch directly on our own professional identity.

The challenges

Many therapists are trained to listen for emotion. We are often rewarded, both implicitly and explicitly, by moments of catharsis, insight, resonance, or expressive release. When those markers are absent, it can be unsettling.

Therapists may feel:

- Flat or disconnected, as though the work isn't landing
- Unproductive, especially if progress isn't showing in traditional emotional terms

- Stuck, unsure how to deepen the process without emotional content
- Tempted to over-interpret, filling the silence with imagined insight
- Anxious to "rescue" the work, by nudging the client towards emotional expression

These feelings are human, but they are also signals, opportunities to reflect on what we expect therapy to look like, and what we assume progress must feel like.

A shift in perspective

Instead of tracking change through emotional insight or increased feeling vocabulary, look for other forms of movement:

- Behavioural change - Is the client responding differently in stressful situations? Are they experimenting with new coping strategies or boundaries?
- Decreased distress - Is there less overwhelm, reactivity, or somatic discomfort, even if the client can't name their emotional state?
- Increased relational connection or self-advocacy - Is the client better able to express needs, tolerate relational vulnerability, or say, "I don't know how I feel, but I want to understand"?

These are meaningful outcomes, they reflect increased self-awareness, emotional regulation, and therapeutic alliance, all without relying on verbalised emotion.

Clients with alexithymia challenge us to become more attuned, more creative, and more spacious in our work. They call us to:

- Trust slower processes

- Hold space without immediate insight
- Value silence as presence, not absence
- Honour the client's way of knowing, even when it differs from our own

Therapy with alexithymic clients may not look or feel dramatic, but it can be deeply impactful. It asks us to meet the client in their world, without demand and that, ultimately, is the work.

Reflective practice

Use the following questions to deepen your self-awareness and explore how you respond to emotional expression, or the absence of it, in the therapy room. These prompts are designed to uncover assumptions, challenge habitual ways of working, and support adaptation when working with clients who may experience alexithymia.

1. *How do I typically recognise emotional engagement in a client? What cues am I relying on, language, tone, facial expression, bodily movement?*
2. *When a client struggles to name a feeling, what's my immediate internal response? Do I feel frustrated, curious, concerned, disconnected? What does that tell me?*
3. *Do I equate emotional expression with emotional depth? Could I be overlooking quieter, more implicit forms of processing?*
4. *Have I ever misinterpreted a client's silence or vagueness as avoidance or disengagement? What else might have been happening?*
5. *What therapeutic techniques in my current practice rely on emotional literacy? Which ones could be adapted for clients with alexithymia?*

6. *Do I believe that insight must be emotional to be meaningful? How might meaning-making look different when emotion isn't accessible?*
7. *When progress doesn't show up as catharsis or language, how do I measure it? Am I open to redefining therapeutic success?*
8. *How might I rephrase common questions to honour a client's way of experiencing emotion? What could I say instead of "How do you feel?" or "What's coming up for you?"*

These questions are not designed to be answered quickly. Sit with them. Return to them. Let them evolve as your work with neurodivergent clients grows. True attunement comes not from having the right tools, but from holding the right posture: curious, respectful, and open to difference.

Chapter 7

It's all connected

As you've been reading, you may have started to notice a pattern.

Whilst each of the cognitive differences explored in this book can show up on their own, for many people they don't. For many these are multi-layered and interwoven into a unique way of experiencing the world and creating a compounding effect of difference that goes unrecognised in most therapeutic spaces.

When I first learned about aphantasia, I thought I'd found the answer to everything. Suddenly, so much made sense: my inability to visualise, the blankness during guided imagery, the way I had never seen anything behind my closed eyes when I was asked to 'picture' something in my mind.

It was only later that I recognised that my 'bad memory' was something more than that, and that my emotional blankness wasn't because I was "cold and unfeeling". Finding that others could hear sounds in their mind and hear their thoughts was another discovery that made so much of my life make sense.

That realisation was both comforting and overwhelming. Comforting because it explained why therapy had always felt slightly out of reach. Overwhelming because it made me aware of just how little the field understood about people like me.

The more I researched, the clearer it became: these cognitive differences often cluster, and where one is found, others are often hiding in plain sight.

Cognitive clustering and why these differences co-occur

As therapists, we're often trained to view cognitive traits in isolation. We might notice a client who struggles to identify emotion and wonder about alexithymia. We might observe difficulty with visualisation and consider aphantasia. What we're far less prepared for is the intersection, the way these often travel together, forming a quiet cognitive cluster that is far more common than current literature suggests.

Though research on these overlaps is still emerging, anecdotal patterns are undeniable. People who discover one difference in how they process experience often uncover others. A client who realises they can't visualise might, in time, also notice that they can't access or emotionally re-live their life memories. That they've never heard an internal voice or that they struggle to identify their emotions. For many, what begins as a single point of insight becomes a cascade of recognition.

So why do these traits co-occur?

1. Shared neurological pathways

While each touches a different aspect of cognition, neuroscience suggests there may be overlapping neural mechanisms at play. For example:

Aphantasia and anauralia both involve diminished activity in the sensory association areas of the brain, particularly the visual and auditory cortices, when engaging in mental imagery tasks.

Anendophasia and alexithymia are linked to underconnectivity between areas involved in internal speech, interoception, and emotional awareness (such as the anterior cingulate cortex, anterior insula, and prefrontal cortex).

SDAM appears to involve reduced connectivity in the default mode network, particularly in regions associated with self-referential thought and autobiographical memory.

These shared differences in connectivity may not cause one another, but they may reflect a broader variation in how some brains process and integrate internal experience. Rather than being separate, unrelated differences, they may be expressions of a distinct cognitive profile, one that processes the world more through logic, external stimuli, and immediate experience than through internal imagery, language, and felt memory.

2. Feedback loops in self-understanding

In therapy and personal development, awareness of one cognitive difference often triggers a re-evaluation of other experiences. For example:

A person who learns they have aphantasia may begin to examine why parts work has always felt confusing or why visual meditations have never worked.

In trying to reflect on their emotional past, they may realise they don't feel connected to memories in the way others describe, leading them to discover SDAM.

As they examine their thinking style, they might notice they don't "hear" their own thoughts, introducing the possibility of anendophasia.

All of this can make the absence of emotional vocabulary feel more understandable, and more obviously alexithymic in nature.

Each discovery doesn't create the next, but it often *reveals* it. One insight pulls the thread, and suddenly the whole cognitive picture begins to make more sense.

3. Diagnostic and research gaps

Another reason these traits appear together so frequently in self-discovery is because they've largely been missed in formal assessments. They don't fit neatly into diagnostic criteria and they're not part of routine psychometric testing. Until recently, they've had little representation in psychological or therapeutic literature.

As a result, many people have had to piece things together themselves. Online forums, personal blogs, social media threads, and books like this one become the space where patterns emerge and identities form and within those spaces, it quickly becomes clear: aphantasia, SDAM, anauralia, anendophasia, and alexithymia are rarely solitary experiences.

4. Impact on therapy engagement

A client with just one of these differences may face minor friction in therapy but a client with several may find the entire structure of therapy feels misaligned.

Consider the table below and the impact where one or more of these are combined.

Core Challenge	**How It Shows Up in Therapy**	**Common Misinterpretations**	**Better Adaptation**
No mental imagery	Difficulty with visualisation techniques, inner child work, or imagined safe spaces	"Not engaging," "blocked," "resistant to imagination"	Use metaphor, physical objects, or verbal description; avoid reliance on visual imagery
No emotional re-living of autobiographical memory	Can't emotionally access or "feel into" the past; struggles with trauma processing that relies on emotional recall	"Detached," "intellectualising," "dissociated"	Focus on meaning-making, observed impact, present-day patterns
No auditory imagery	Can't hear imagined voices, guided meditations feel empty, difficult to "hear" inner critic	"Not visualising correctly," "inattentive," "not trying"	Remove references to imagined sound; use written prompts or non-auditory cues

No internal monologue	Can't access internal dialogue, parts work falls flat, struggles with journaling	"Shut down," "emotionally shallow," "avoiding the work"	Use instinctive reflection, metaphor, or non-verbal techniques; externalise thoughts through objects or movement
Difficulty identifying and describing emotion	Repeated "I don't know" responses, vague emotional language, somatic descriptions with no affect	"Unemotional," "resistant," "not doing the work"	Validate body-based descriptions; scaffold emotional vocabulary; shift to values-based work

The SDAM chapter offered a live example of why this clustering matters. Whether emotional re-living survives in SDAM appears to vary from person to person, and where alexithymia is also present, the emotional strand is far more likely to be out of reach. Two clients with the same difference on paper can need different doors, which is exactly why the question is never the label, and always what is present for the mind in front of you.

Clients who believe they've failed at therapy

So, what is it like for people with these overlapping differences? Many have had multiple therapists, and they've invested time, energy, and money into healing. They've shown up, done the work, stayed present, and still left feeling unseen.

Some say:

- "I always feel like I'm just not trying hard enough."
- "I nod and go along with it, but nothing happens inside."
- "Everyone else seems to get something out of therapy, I just feel numb."
- "I think I've just resigned myself to managing on my own."

These are not unmotivated clients, and they are not emotionally shut down. They are simply people whose minds don't match the methods.

Most of them had no idea why therapy wasn't working for them, because no one had ever explained that their internal experience might be cognitively different.

That's why so many of them come to this knowledge late. They discover terms like *aphantasia* or *alexithymia* by accident, often online, and then experience a moment of profound recognition.

The power of one question

When I reflect on all the therapists I saw before understanding my own cognitive profile, there's one question I wish just one of them had asked what my inner world was like.

Not "Can you visualise a safe place?" Not "What does your inner child look like?" Just: "How do you experience thought, memory, and emotion?"

That question would have opened a door. It would have invited me to describe my actual experience, rather than try to fit into theirs.

Therapists often feel pressure to *do* something when therapy isn't moving but sometimes the most powerful shift comes not from action, but from genuine curiosity.

When a therapist slows down enough to ask, and then *believe*, they create space for the client to stop performing, start expressing, and finally feel seen.

The emotional toll of being misunderstood

The cumulative impact of being repeatedly misunderstood in therapy is hard to quantify.

For clients, it can look like: Masking during sessions; retreating into silence; avoiding future help; feeling ashamed of their differences and believing they are "not fixable" or "too broken" to benefit from support.

For therapists, it can create a quiet sense of failure that can have them asking questions like: "Why isn't this landing?" "What am I missing?" "Maybe I'm not the right therapist for them." "They're just not ready for the work "When you bring these overlapping differences into focus, you start to understand how they interact, and you no longer need to guess.

You start to see that the mismatch wasn't between therapist and client but between assumption and reality.

Reena's story

Reena, a 41-year-old creative director, came to therapy reporting "generalised burnout," difficulty connecting with others, and a sense that "nothing ever sticks." She described herself as high functioning but emotionally flat. "I'm productive, I meet deadlines, I manage people well, but inside, it's like there's nothing there," she said in her first session.

Her therapist initially suspected unresolved trauma or emotional avoidance. Reena struggled to answer questions about how she felt, what she remembered about past emotional events, or how her inner critic sounded. She offered phrases like:

"I know something happened, but I don't really feel anything about it." "I don't talk to myself in my head, it's just quiet." "I feel things physically more than emotionally, but I can't explain what those feelings are."

Over the first few weeks, several therapy interventions fell flat and Reena felt like she was just "playing along".

Eventually, she said something that changed the course of therapy:

"Do most people really see things in their mind? Like, pictures? Because I've never been able to do that."

This prompted her therapist to explore further, gently asking about her internal experience:

- *"When you remember something, do you see it like a movie or more like a list?"*

- *"Do you hear your own voice in your head when you think?"*
- *"If something upsets you, do you know what emotion you're feeling, or do you just feel off?"*

It was the first time anyone had asked those questions.

She answered that she didn't see anything, she didn't hear her own voice, and she didn't know what she was feeling most of the time, just that her stomach would tighten, or her jaw would ache.

Together, they began to identify a cognitive cluster: that had shaped her entire life and yet gone unnamed. Her previous experiences in therapy now made sense.

Once this was understood, therapy shifted to metaphor, external tools, and values-based reflection. They explored her experiences through pattern recognition, behavioural insights, and collaborative sense-making and Reena started to flourish and the silence in her mind became a space for clarity.

By the end of therapy, Reena hadn't found a voice in her head, but she'd found her own voice in the room.

From feeling broken to feeling understood

The moment I discovered that there was nothing *wrong* with me, that my mind simply worked differently, everything changed.

I stopped trying to visualise what wasn't there. I stopped looking for a voice I'd never had. I stopped pushing myself to feel memories I couldn't access, and I started asking better questions. I started designing different tools and I started adapting practices to match *my* way of experiencing the world.

Eventually, I created the training I wish my former therapists had had, because they were unprepared and because no one had taught them that these differences exist, let alone how to respond to them.

That's the shift I hope this book begins for you. Not to make you an expert overnight and not to replace your current knowledge, but to layer in something new, something essential. A way of working with clients who have always been in the room, just quietly misunderstood.

Therapy that works at the edges

When the standard tools don't land, we might assume the work has stalled. We reach for better questions, sharper formulations, more precise interventions. When a client's internal world doesn't match the assumptions baked into our models, though, refinement alone won't fix the mismatch. What's needed is something more fundamental: a willingness to work at the edge of what therapy usually asks.

Clients with clustered cognitive differences often live at those edges. They think without imagery, recall without emotion, feel without language, and know without words. Their experiences fall outside the norms of visualisation, emotional recall, inner speech, or narrative coherence. Yet their therapeutic needs are just as valid, and often just as urgent.

So how do we support them?

Step one: adapt the framework, not the client

When imagery, parts work, or emotional re-living doesn't work, the instinct is often to persist, or to interpret non-response as avoidance. Instead, pause and reassess. Ask: *Is this a client who processes differently?*

If so, shift your expectations. Move from internal to external. From expressive to observational. From imagined scenes to grounded moments. From "What does it feel like?" to "What does it do in your life?"

Here are a few reframes you might consider:

Instead of...	**Try asking...**
"Can you picture a safe place?"	"When you think of safety, what comes to mind? Maybe a word, a person, a place, or a sensation?"
"What's your inner critic saying?"	"How do you know when you're being hard on yourself?"
"Where do you feel that in your body?"	"Do you notice any shifts or sensations when this comes up?"
"What's coming up emotionally?"	"If you had to describe this feeling with a word or metaphor, what might fit?"
"Let's journal about this part of you."	"Would it help to write this out, draw it, or talk through it together?"

Step two: work with what's available

Clients with these traits still have access to something rich. It may be:

- Somatic data: tension, sensation, gesture
- Behavioural patterns: how they move through the world
- Values and choices: what they care about, even if they can't explain why
- Symbolic expression: metaphor, analogy, or image-making
- Systems-level awareness: logic, insight, clarity of impact

Therapy becomes less about uncovering what's buried, and more about noticing what's already in motion. The work is in naming, refining, and strengthening what's present, not chasing what isn't.

Step three: let silence be a language

A client who doesn't speak from an inner voice or re-live emotion may still be deeply reflective, but their reflection might happen in stillness and in slowness. In sideways insights that emerge unexpectedly. When we rush to fill that space, we miss it.

Let the silence stretch a little longer to allow the knowing to arrive another way.

When therapists stop trying to "fix" the gaps and start collaborating with the client's actual mode of processing, something powerful happens. The therapy begins to fit, because you stopped asking the client to walk into your world, and chose, instead, to meet them in theirs.

Small shifts to start today

Here are five simple ways to begin creating more inclusive sessions:

1. Add one question to your intake form: *"Do you experience thoughts as images, words, feelings, or something else?"*
2. Pause when a technique doesn't land: Instead of repeating the prompt, try asking: *"Would another approach feel easier to access right now?"*
3. Offer alternatives to visualisation: Use metaphor, sensation, or description, not just imagery.
4. Stay curious about emotional processing: If a client can't name a feeling, try scaling, colour coding, or body-mapping.
5. Normalise difference: Say aloud: *"There are lots of ways people experience their inner world. There's no right or wrong way."*

These aren't revolutionary changes, but for the right client, they can change everything.

Therapists are trained to develop hypotheses, to sense what might be happening under the surface and that's a powerful skill, but it can also backfire when our projections are based on how *we* process experience, rather than how *our client* does.

Inclusive practice asks us to hold our insight lightly and check in more often. To replace projection with precision.

Instead of: "They didn't react. Maybe they're avoiding." Try: "They didn't react. Could it be they process internally in a different way?"

Instead of: "They couldn't access that memory. Maybe it's repressed." Try: "Could their memory function differently?"

Precision doesn't mean clinical coldness. It means tailoring our assumptions with care. It means staying open to the possibility that the client's mind works in ways we were never taught to expect.

A small shift, a big impact

Sometimes the shift is subtle. A small change in question. A moment of validation. A choice to pause rather than press on.

One therapist told me about a client who "never seemed to get" visualisation exercises. After reading about aphantasia, she asked the client directly whether they were able to form mental images. The client looked relieved and said, "No. I thought I was just doing it wrong all these years."

They both laughed. Then they began working with words and metaphor instead of scenes. It wasn't revolutionary. It was simply right for that client and that's the shift.

Practice externalising the internal experience. Externalising makes the abstract concrete. It gives form to what can't be pictured or narrated internally. For some clients, it opens the door to emotional exploration they'd previously assumed was closed.

Why it matters systemically

This isn't just about one client at a time. When we expand our awareness of cognitive difference, we begin to challenge a much broader issue in psychotherapy: the quiet privileging of certain minds.

Therapy has long favoured:

- The reflective narrator

- The emotionally articulate client
- The imaginative visualiser
- The metaphor-friendly thinker

What about the logical analyst, the fact-based observer or the quiet processor who can't see, hear, or feel internally the way most models assume?

They've been unintentionally overlooked.

Inclusive practice pushes back. It says: There is no one right way to be a client and if our models can't stretch to include those differences, maybe it's time to stretch the models.

Don't worry that you're not yet an expert.

This book hasn't asked you to memorise a new set of diagnostic criteria. It hasn't handed you a list of ten things to do in every session. It certainly hasn't tried to teach you everything there is to know about these differences.

That's because inclusive practice doesn't begin with expertise. It begins with orientation.

You don't have to get it perfect. You just have to get curious.

From now on, you can pause before offering an intervention and ask, *"Will this land for this client?"* You can ask at intake, *"How do you experience your inner world: through pictures, sounds, words, or something else?"* You can say, *"If this exercise doesn't work for you, we'll find something that does."*

It's a start. To deepen your understanding and gain practical tools for adapting your work, becoming an Unseen Minds Practitioner® is the natural next step.

Reflective practice

1. *Think of one client who disengaged. With this new lens, how might you reimagine what was happening?*
2. *Revisit your assumptions about therapeutic resistance. Could difference, not defiance, have been the underlying cause?*
3. *What would you do differently now, knowing what you know about these overlapping traits?*
4. *Reflect on the last time you asked a client to "go back," "talk to a part," or "name what they feel. "How might you ask that differently next time?*
5. *How might your intake or assessment process change in light of what you've learned?*
6. *What are three therapeutic techniques you use often? What do they assume about internal experience?*

Chapter 8

What comes next?

By now, you've encountered a different kind of client story, and you've seen what it means to live without inner imagery, to remember without emotional pull, to think without an internal voice and to feel without the language to describe it.

You've walked through case examples, listened in on the quiet cues, and begun to recognise how standard therapy can miss the mark, not because clients aren't engaging, but because we've never been taught to recognise how *they* engage.

This chapter is here to pause and to hold up the mirror rather than re-teach what you've already learned. If you're like most reflective practitioners, you're already starting to ask yourself some important questions.

- *Have I worked with clients like this and not realised it?*
- *Have I ever misinterpreted silence, vagueness, or disconnection?*
- *What might have changed if I'd understood what was actually happening?*

This is the therapist's turning point. The moment not of critique, but of clarity.

What you might be feeling right now

When reading this book, a quiet discomfort might have begun to settle in around this point. You might be remembering a client who drifted away, one who always felt "hard to reach", or someone you struggled to connect with despite doing everything you'd been taught.

If that's you, please hear this clearly: none of it is your fault. Most training programmes don't mention these cognitive differences at all. They're absent from the literature, from clinical supervision, from case formulations and from CPD events. You weren't taught how to spot this. Now that you know, you can choose to go deeper.

What this means for CPD and clinical training

That's what continuing professional development is meant to offer: not just more tools, but deeper clarity. A way to work more effectively, more ethically, and with greater attunement to the full range of human experience.

These cognitive differences challenge some of the foundational assumptions in therapy. They expose the gaps where our training has often been silent, about how thought, memory, imagination and feeling actually work.

So, what do we do with that knowledge? We build on it, we expand our frame, and we invest in training that helps us include the clients we've unintentionally left out.

The next step, if you want one

This book carries the name Unseen Minds for a reason, and so does the training that grew from it. The Unseen Minds Practitioner® (Therapist Track) is the CPD-accredited specialist credential I built for exactly the questions this book has raised. It's a reorientation as much as a resource, a space to explore, practise and apply what you've begun to glimpse in these pages. Inside the programme, we go further into:

- Clinical adaptations
- Therapy models that work without internal imagery or dialogue
- Ethical practice for cognitive inclusion
- Case study supervision and client communication strategies
- Opportunities to reflect on your own cognitive processing style

The training supports you to develop the tools for the clients who are already in your practice, whether or not you knew they were there. It's about becoming the therapist who no longer says, "I don't know why this isn't working," but instead says, "Ah, I see you now. Let's find a way that works for you." For a client who has spent their whole life feeling like therapy is something that happens to other people, that moment of recognition can be life changing.

You'll find the full details at aphantasiaacademy.com.

If you'd like to start smaller

Specialist training is a commitment, and you may want to test the water first. My free masterclass, CBT For Invisible Cognitive Differences, is the natural starting point: a focused look at where cognitive barriers show up inside CBT and related tools, and the first step many Unseen Minds Practitioners took. From there, Aphantasia Foundations gives you a clear grounding in all five differences before specialist practice, and the code FOUNDATIONS50 gives you £50 off as a reader of this book. Whichever step fits, you'll find them both at aphantasiaacademy.com/book.

If you work within a service or organisation

Some of you will be reading this inside NHS Talking Therapies, a university or student support team, an EAP, a charity or a counselling organisation, where the clients keep coming but the training decisions sit elsewhere. I deliver bespoke awareness training, workshops and consultancy for teams like yours, built around the realities of your service rather than a one-size-fits-all deck. If this book has named something you're seeing across your caseloads, share it with your service lead, or get in touch through the website and we'll talk about what your team needs.

If this book is where you stop

Some readers will close this book and go no further, and I want to say plainly that this is enough. You now know what most therapists were never taught. Asking one open question about how a client's mind works, or adapting one exercise that quietly relied on imagery, will change someone's experience of therapy, and you can do both tomorrow without a single further qualification. If the book has been useful, the kindest thing you can do with it is mention it to a colleague. Every therapist who understands these differences means more clients who are no longer unseen.

Thank you

This book began with a story, my story. A story of therapy that didn't land, of being asked to visualise, to recall, to speak to an inner voice I didn't have. Of feeling unseen not just by people in my life, but by the very professionals I turned to for support. It also began with a belief that therapists are some of the most compassionate, curious, and capable people I know and that with the right knowledge and tools, you can change lives like mine.

That you took the time to buy and read this book means the world to me. In doing so I know that, together, we will help people like me to feel safe, seen and heard.

As a thank you, the code UNSEENMINDS gives you £100 off the full Unseen Minds Practitioner® training at checkout. Access this by on the website aphantasiaacademy.com/book

My particular thanks to Neil Kimmelfield, whose generous correspondence after the first edition deepened this book's understanding of SDAM.

Thank you.

Further reading and information

Galton, F. (1880). Statistics of mental imagery. *Mind*, https://galton.org/essays/1880-1889/galton-1880-mind-statistics-mental-imagery.pdf

Zeman, A., Dewar, M. and Della Sala, S. (2015). Lives without imagery – Congenital aphantasia. *Cortex*, 73, pp.378–380. https://www.sciencedirect.com/science/article/abs/pii/S0010945215001781?via%3Dihub

Pearson, J. (2024). The shocking ways aphantasia can change how you think and feel. [YouTube Video]. Available at: https://www.youtube.com/watch?v=V_-HZvrdhQM

Mawtus, B., Renwick, F., Thomas, B.R. and Reeder, R.R. (2024). The impact of aphantasia on mental healthcare experiences. *Collabra: Psychology*, 10(1), 127416. https://doi.org/10.1525/collabra.127416

Palombo, D.J., Sheldon, S. and Levine, B. (2018). Individual differences in autobiographical memory. *Trends in Cognitive Sciences*, 22(7), pp.583–597. https://doi.org/10.1016/j.tics.2018.04.007

Monzel, M., Karneboge, J. and Reuter, M. (2024). Affective processing in aphantasia and potential overlaps with alexithymia: Mental imagery facilitates the recognition of emotions in oneself and others. *Biomarkers in Neuropsychiatry*, 11, 100106. https://doi.org/10.1016/j.bionps.2024.100106

Karukivi, M. and Saarijärvi, S. (2014). Development of alexithymic personality features. *World Journal of Psychiatry*, 4(4), pp.91–102. https://doi.org/10.5498/wjp.v4.i4.91

Dance, C.J., Ipser, A. and Simner, J. (2022). The prevalence of aphantasia (imagery weakness) in the general population. *Consciousness and Cognition*, 97, 103243. https://doi.org/10.1016/j.concog.2021.103243

Dance, C.J., Jaquiery, M., Eagleman, D.M., Porteous, D. and Simner, J. (2021). What is the relationship between aphantasia, synaesthesia and autism? *Consciousness and Cognition*, 89, 103087. https://doi.org/10.1016/j.concog.2021.103087

Hinwar, R.P. and Lambert, A.J. (2021). Anauralia: The silent mind and its association with aphantasia. *Frontiers in Psychology*, 12, 744213. https://doi.org/10.3389/fpsyg.2021.744213

Nedergaard, J.S.K. and Lupyan, G. (2024). Not everybody has an inner voice: Behavioural consequences of anendophasia.

Psychological Science, 35(7), pp.780–797.

https://doi.org/10.1177/09567976241252515

Made in the USA
Monee, IL
14 September 2026

63129447R00083